The Hotel on
St. James Place

The Hotel on St. James Place

**Growing up in Atlantic City
between the Boardwalk
and the Holocaust**

Molly Golubcow

Bartleby Press
Washington • Baltimore

ISBN 978-0935437-57-7

Library of Congress Control Number: 2020947058

Cover design by Ross Feldner

Published by:

Bartleby Press

PO Box 858
Savage, Maryland 20763
800-953-9929
www.BartlebythePublisher.com

Printed in the United States of America

10 9 8 7 6 5 4 3

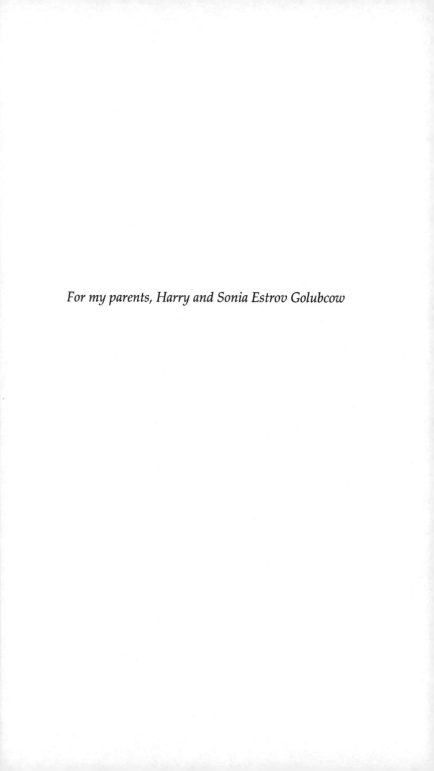

For my parents, Harry and Sonia Estrov Golubcow

Contents

Contents

Chapter One

Fisher & Scootie

As the owner of a small hotel, frequented by lost souls who had a little bit of money and maybe a police record or two, my father sat behind the high-gloss lacquered desk of the New Seacrest Hotel in Atlantic City, New Jersey. With his head slightly tilted and chin cupped in his right hand, he tried not to fall asleep late at night. It never dawned on me then that my father didn't seem to need sleep like the rest of us—horizontal, under covers, tucked away safe and sound. My friends would ask him with teasing curiosity, "Mr. G, when do you ever go to sleep?" To which he would always reply in his own Yiddish version of English: "In the vinter time after the summer ven business is slow, I vill sleep."

It was making a joke, but there was something dark

behind the humor. Never really a sound sleeper, regardless of the season, the night provided too many opportunities for my father to again see the horrors. Families, along with his own, children, mothers, teachers, neighbors, an entire ghetto showered upon by a downpour of machine gun fire conducted by the wave of a leather-gloved hand of the SS. Then, the spraying of bullets and the screaming. Most were instantly dead, others slowly dying, and a handful of living—scattered and blood-drenched without a damn of protection from the heavens or a single human being.

In the Spring of 1945, twenty-five years before my father sat sentry at the Seacrest Hotel, Hitler cyanided his prize shepherd, Blondi, a final shame to add to his long list, before he and wife Ava partook of the same poison. The war had finally ended, leaving the survivors to sort through the wreckage of their lives and memories; at least try to make sense of unspeakable days, months, and years full of humanity sinking ever lower. They resolved to *never forget the 6 million Jews murdered.* And, vowed to go on just to spite the bastards that dreamed of mastering the races in the first place.

For my father, the journey to Atlantic City, New Jersey was not a direct or even desired route from Miory, Poland, a small town 114 miles north of Minsk in present day Belarus.

It began in earnest in 1942 as the ghetto was being eliminated, liquidated, annihilated, and destroyed. Forced to go outside to be "counted" yet again, the 220 ghetto dwellers were herded out to the open field by the Krukefke woods. And then the events of this day suddenly became clear. Nazis barking out orders to undress, line up. *Shnell, Shnell!* Children crying, clutching mothers. Aged men reciting the *Shema* prayer. Tears smoothly rolled down cheeks as a precursor to the blood that would soon flow.

When I was a teenager, I would ask my father about that day. Like a prosecutor, my questions were direct and at times relentless. "Why didn't you just punch a Nazi?" I would ask. "How come a bunch of people didn't just resist—fight, push, something?"

He would exhale and try to explain a horror that only someone who was there could possibly comprehend. He would lean back into his chair, look straight across the table almost looking beyond me as if he were watching a movie screen and say, "It's easy to say when we're sitting here what I should have done—when it happened, we were all like walking dead people already—no hope, broken." Most of the time I accepted what seemed an unsatisfying explanation, but left my father to his memories of the last moments with his first family.

That morning, every Jew in Miory recalled the words recited every year in *shul* at Yom Kippur. *Who shall live and who shall die? Who by fire, who by drowning, who by wild beast?* Suddenly each word rose from the pages of the holy *machzor* and took shape. Not a Jewish soul was spared the horror of witnessing words so holy, so routinely said year after year, come to life on a cloudy day in May of 1942. Every Jew stood and watched their judgment instantly administered to the 220.

The long bearded *rebbe*, the first to be shot against the knurled oak. The Yeshiva *bocher* who planned to study the words of God for the rest of his life. The tailor's daughter who never married because of her clubfoot and now never would. Babies wrapped in blankets crying for milk, children who played their last game of jacks that morning, old men, young lovers, wealthy, poor, wise, ignorant, all fell like paper-crisp leaves in Autumn into the pre-dug mass grave.

Where one body began and another ended was not clearly defined since blood and dirt sullied each person's uniqueness. What was once a small vibrant *shtetel* morphed into a mass of naked, pale skins on soft baby bellies, gray learned beards, blonde hair like flax, arthritic fingers, and hazel eyes, closed forever—all covered with blood flowing in and out.

My father survived because of God. Not necessarily because of the concept of the almighty but the word "God" itself. When the purpose of the Nazis and the future of all the naked humiliated souls became clear to him, my father cried out, "*Mine Gott.*"

His prayer was immediately answered with a rifle butt to the left side of his head and a response from one of Hitler Youth's finest, "You have no God, he's ours." He fell to the ground before the bullets began- old, young, good, and even bad souls went up to the heavens en masse.

My father laid unconscious by the giant hole in the ground. When he awoke, nothing was moving; even blood had stopped flowing and began crusting on the dead. He staggered into the dark woods where not even a partial moon shed some light on what had happened and what would happen next. All he knew for certain was that his entire family, part of the exodus direct to heaven that afternoon, left him alive and behind. He spent the rest of the war in those woods with a band of Polish Resistance fighters imagining the touch of his wife, the smile of his teenage daughter, and the sound of his eight-year-old son calling him *Tateh*.

October of 1945 was the time for survivors to trickle back to wherever home was before the world went mad. And like teenagers at a school dance, those who migrated back to their hometowns awkwardly paired up because mustering all their strength to go on was the only thing they could do. That was how my parents met—not at the shake shop or at a high school dance, like most of my friends' parents, but at a gathering of Miory survivors.

My parents knew each other before the war. Miory was such a small town, the Jewish population in 1921 was 371 people. Sonia, my mother, was the second cousin of Malkeh, my father's first wife. Because of their mutual losses, they and the other survivors spent many evenings reviewing the list of those who perished, where, and how. Bits and pieces of the horror put together the sorry picture—15 out of 220 survived. The small group would meet and reminisce, a typical evening in Miory in 1945, about friends and family never to be seen again. And for the living, where to go from here.

As my mother sat one evening with Dvayrel, Bocher, and some of the others who were either lucky or unlucky to have survived, she remembered a beautiful afternoon in Miory and a walk with her cousin Malkeh four years before the war started. The air was crisp; winter was beginning. The two strolled across the wooden bridge over the creek.

Malkeh was several years older than Sonia, but they enjoyed each other's company. Sonia, who was one of seven poor children, loved to hear about the warmth and love and beautiful things her cousin possessed—a happy marriage, two wonderful children, and a lovely home. As they crossed the bridge Malkeh put up her collar to shield the breeze that was beginning to blow a little harder than when they began their walk.

Malkeh suddenly stopped walking and confided to Sonia that she was having bad dreams—similar themes telling her that she wouldn't live a long life with the husband she adored. She couldn't remember all the details of her dreams, but a vision of her family destroyed by several faceless men with guns replayed to her. Malkeh's voice trembled as she asked Sonia, as if it were a normal request, "Can you help me knit a shawl?" Would Sonia marry her husband when she dies?

My mother blushed and stuttered. She assured Malkeh that her dreams were silly—nothing more than bad dreams. In fact, she told Malkeh that her dreams may have been caused by that man who came to their town and delivered a scary message. He was a Zionist from Israel, one of Ze'ev Jabotinsky's people warning the townspeople that a "volcano was about to erupt..."

My father attended that meeting in 1938. The man, eager to entice Jews to immigrate to Palestine or even Madagascar—an intermediary plan Jabotinsky and Chaim Weizmann were proposing since the British were not keen on allowing Jews into British held Palestine, delivered a powerful speech. He warned them that this impending tragedy would be worse than an occasional pogrom when some drunken Poles had too much to drink and needed a Jew to beat up or a Jewish house or barn to burn down,

My father remembered the Zionist's exact words In Yiddish:

"Jews, a fire is burning beneath your feet—run, escape now!"

Although my father did not find the concept of Jews returning to the homeland unappealing—"Next year in Jerusalem," after all it as is said every year at the Seder table on Passover, he thought uprooting his family and business to go to a desert was not anything he would do at that point in his life. I don't know if my father discussed the meeting's warnings with Malkeh. However, the word got around and even my mother, a young teenager at the time, knew about the Zionist's warning. As she listened to Malkeh and her strange request, the thought of a wealthy man having any interest in a poor child 13 years younger than she would have made her laugh out loud if her cousin did not look so serious. The snow began to fall and the two hurried home. The conversation ended, forgotten until that evening in what was left of the town of Miory, Poland.

After a few months of small gatherings and mourning the lost, my parents married and her cousin Malkeh's dreams eerily woke into reality. The new family came to America on July 4th, 1950 with a son who was born in the Bad Reichenhall Displaced Persons camp near Salzburg Germany in the American Occupation Zone.

In keeping with Ashkenazi tradition, my brother, Saul, was named after my mother's father who was killed in the war. Ten years later, I was born in Vineland, New Jersey. I was named Malkeh, after my father's first wife. For Holocaust survivors starting new families, names were bountiful in the late 40s and early 50s. Harry and Sonia were my parents. Saul was my brother. A new family on a chicken farm in Vineland where dozens of other Holocaust survivors found new homes. *"…We shall never forget…."*

The Seacrest was the second hotel my family operated. I

was in fourth grade when we left Vineland—small farms were struggling by the mid-1960s and becoming a thing of the past. At the suggestion of several Holocaust survivors who had already moved into the hotel business, my parents rented an entire hotel on Park Place, across from the classic Claridge Hotel. Similar to a rent with an option to buy deal, my parents operated the hotel from Memorial Day to Labor Day; getting their feet wet, literally and figuratively, steps away from the beach and Boardwalk.

I was only nine years old, and the Cheltenham Hotel, a wooden structure from the 1930s with a wraparound porch and tired green awnings, was a fun place to play even though I had to leave my dog, Lassie, back on the farm until September. My brother stayed on the farm and worked at the Kimble Glass Company earning money to pay for his college tuition. I'm not sure if my parents were scared of the new venture they were trying out. Like most kids, I was oblivious to their fears and concerns; or maybe they did their best to keep the anxiety out of my narrow world.

When guests would check in, I would play bellhop accompanying them to their rooms, which almost always earned me at least 25 cents since they thought my attempts to carry a small bag were so cute. That payoff guaranteed me several hours of pinball at the neighboring Empress Motel. The game featured a Spanish Flamenco dancer brightly displayed in the back glass whose fan slats would fold out with a loud click each time I hit a bonus round.

Across the street from the Cheltenham, limos chauffeured fancy ladies in gowns and furs and men in tuxedos, who never even noticed the Cheltenham draped in the shadow of the Claridge. I made friends with the drivers who let the little kid from across the street play in the limos when they were not in use. What a thrill it was to sit in the back seat and play with the radio dials hearing The Supremes telling me that you can't hurry love. The only restriction from the drivers was to "stay away from the booze" in Sammy Davis's black Cadillac limo—silver and black chrome interior with leopard pillows.

After a successful year at the Cheltenham, my parents sold the farm in Vineland and we moved to Atlantic City. They rented out hotels for the summer season two more years before they bought the Seacrest in 1970. During the school year, we lived in a three-bedroom apartment facing the beach on Atlantic and Jackson Avenue on the Ventnor side. The north side of Jackson Avenue was Atlantic City and the other side was Ventnor.

Once school ended, I looked forward to going to the hotel. For me it was a welcome break from residential life—time to breathe air that was not so tame. Ventnor was only two miles away from the hotel in Atlantic City, but hundreds of miles away in its definition of life.

Every day in Atlantic City brought a world to get lost

in for a teenager—penny auctions with a shill planted in the third row, frozen custard swirled in a chocolate/vanilla braid, miniature golf courses, Mr. Peanut giving away plastic bank replicas of himself, and fortune tellers who couldn't read a word in a newspaper, but were scholarly with a palm if it held a $5 bill. Boardwalk arcades clanged with the sounds of 10-cent pinball machines as the Italian ice vendor pawned his wares. On the corner of St. James Place and the Boardwalk, the neon sign advertising the Seacrest Hotel could be seen half way down the block with the "L" flashing and hissing throughout the night.

If the street, St. James Place, sounds familiar, it is one of the three—along with Tennessee Avenue and New York Avenue—orange properties on the Monopoly board.

And so, the summer proceeded. My father sat behind the front desk always ready to check a customer in or out. Hundreds of people would pass by his desk throughout the summer. Some arrived with enthusiasm, but would leave with disappointment; a child that couldn't be convinced to get off the streets and come home, a drunk that couldn't give up his self-made hell, a husband and wife who gave up on trying to make their marriage work. Others were down so low when they checked-in, the Seacrest became their haven.

Scootie was one of those souls. She sold herself every night on Pacific Avenue so she could supply her needle with sweet liquid to soothe her veins. Fisher was her pimp.

One morning she decided to stop by becoming a cliché of someone who hits rock bottom and assesses "What the hell am I doing to myself?" She had to choose between drowning in her life's juices or breaking out and away from a pimp and a needle. My father helped her come to that conclusion without having to say a single word to her.

One particular morning, I was woken by a woman's terrified shriek. *Was it a dream?* My eyes opened and I tried to calculate what was real. It was too light out to be night and still too dark to be morning; the time when Scootie handed over her earnings to Fisher. A crashing noise was next, then the organic sound of a hand slapping against a face, followed by another scream. The sounds seemed to be coming from the lobby. I knew my father was out there, so I jolted out of bed and ran towards the screaming. The pea-green ceramic lamp with the flower cut-outs lampshade was shattered on the floor. Scootie's belongings were scattered across the lobby.

"Stop it, you're hurting her." My mother was already pleading with Fisher to stop strangling Scootie. My father kept yelling out Fisher's name as if hearing his name would somehow jog some kind of humanity within him and make him stop.

Fisher was a tall menacing man, even on the rare occasions when he smiled. Scootie's pink plastic ball earrings swung back and forth with each squeeze of her neck and banged against his pinkie ring, a large gold "F" within a circle of diamonds. His strong hands, muscles tensed with a mission, were wrapped around Scootie's neck as she gasped for any iota of air she could find. Like a Tango dip, her body was bent backwards in a slight curve. He held her upright by the neck with his grip while strangling her at the same time. If it weren't for the fact that Fisher was murdering Scootie, their pose looked choreographed.

I remembered the first time I saw Fisher and Scootie. They checked into room twenty-nine as Mr. and Mrs. Fisher, rarely speaking a word to each other. He was tall, pushing six feet, very lean and muscular. Scootie, whose mocha skin looked almost pale next to his dark, bittersweet chocolate complexion, spent her afternoons sitting on the couch in the lobby eating cream filled Tasty-Cakes while watching cartoons on the television. Many times, she would bite into the cupcake with her ruby lipstick lips, and fall asleep mid bite. She was always calm, mellow, and quiet. Especially when Fisher was close by. My mother thought Scootie was drunk—I assumed she was high—and supplied by Fisher as a reward for turning enough tricks the night before.

One afternoon, Fisher went to make a call in the spray-painted gold phone booth in the lobby. He slowly walked toward the phone with a gait that came from life on the streets. He closed the folding door in the booth carefully and deliberately. Even though the sound was muffled, I could hear every word he said. I was reading a magazine in the lounge chair next to the phone booth.

The dime clanged into the phone and I heard the rotary dialing a number.

Most of the conversation consisted of "a-ha" and "nah" and an occasional grunt. Then, the only full sentence I heard him say was, "Look, I killed before and I ain't got no problem killin' again."

Fisher would pay his rent weekly in cash with money that Scootie earned for him. He'd ask my father how business was going, my father would reciprocate and ask about his, and a word or two about the weather. It wasn't that my father approved of Fisher's work and methods. Fisher was a man who had no respect for a single soul on earth. Life was cheap. But for some reason, they understood each other. They both learned that circumstances throw people together that don't necessarily seem destined to meet whether it's in an alley, a bus, a marriage; anywhere.

"Hitler was a strange matchmaker," my father would always comment about the new life and the world he and the other survivors were thrust into. He used that sentence in Yiddish on many occasions to explain people he knew that just didn't seem to make sense together—like plaids and stripes—clashing instead of matching. "*Hitler is geven a modner shadchun...*"

That morning in the lobby, Scootie's wide-open eyes were rimmed with a blackish blend of tears and mascara that streaked down her face. My father ran over to Fisher and shouted his name again. A short, stocky man, my father looked dwarfed next to Fisher's long, angry body. *Here we go again* my father must have thought. *Tears and screaming and a monster killing in front of me—again. I thought this was 1972; the Nazis were destroyed. But, here I am wide-awake, with demons before me.* Again, my father yelled Fisher's name in a much deeper serious tone. But this time he added, "Fisher, it's not nice to do this in a lobby. Go to your room and do this."

It was a surreal moment. *Was my father joking?* This was not a time for humor. *Was he concerned that a strangled woman in the lobby would be bad for business?* This was not a time to think of business. It seemed to take some time for that sentence to translate into all of our minds. You could almost see Fisher digesting the words as he ever so slowly turned and looked at my father with a completely puzzled look on his sweaty face. In that split second of distraction, Scootie broke away and ran behind the front desk. My mother whisked her into the kitchen. My father pushed Fisher outside onto the porch to calm him down, and just like that it was all over.

I'm certain that my father saved Scootie from dying that morning; something he couldn't do years earlier for his own family. For nearly thirty years, he replayed the ghetto liquidation scene in Miory, Poland over and over in his head, but could never figure out how he could have saved them, all of them, some of them, not even one of them. That day in the lobby of the Seacrest my father saved a life without having to fight or hurt anyone else. Perhaps he was due a win. More likely, it was more of a lucky day for Scootie, than my father. Later, I saw Scootie in the phone booth. The very next day, a man who looked like he could have been her father arrived and took her away.

Fisher lived at the Seacrest for a few more weeks, moving out at the end of the summer. A year later, we saw him again. It was Yom Kippur, the Day of Atonement, the day God seals our fate in the book of life for another year. *Who shall live and who shall die? Who by fire and who by thirst? Who by water? Who by wild beasts?* It was a long day. We were eager to get home, have my mother's *lekech* (honey cake) and a glass of tea to break the fast.

As we exited the massive doors of Rodef Shalom, the old synagogue on Pacific Avenue, Fisher happened to walk by. He ran over and shook hands with my father.

"How's business?" my father asked him. They chatted for a few minutes. An Atlantic City policeman, directing traffic, stared with a bewildered look trying to figure out how these two men could have ever known each other. Fisher patted my father on the back and wished him well. My family went back to the hotel. Fisher walked down the street and turned into a corner bar. My father was right, "Hitler was a strange matchmaker."

Chapter Two

Artie & Harvey

Every Monday through Friday, 8-4, Artie Winters swept up pulp scraps that fell to the shop floor at the Tacony papermill in South Philadelphia. By 5:05, he walked home two blocks where his 72-year-old mother had dinner waiting for him in their row house, second from the end on Lehigh Avenue.

From the day he was born, Mrs. Winters referred to her son as "...a special gift from God." She never came to the hotel, but Mrs. Winters would call on occasion—rare occasions not to run up her long distance phone bill, to check up on her son. My mother would end up chatting with her and hearing stories about her "little Artie" conceived late in life from a short-lived marriage. As Mrs.Winters would always tell my mother, "I knew when I first held him in my arms, that Arthur Mason Winters II would always be a bit 'slow in the head.'" So, she made sure his life was always simple and routine. On Saturday, she would launder and iron her son's blue uniform as well as his regular clothes - white button-down shirts and black polyester-blend pants – size 42 to accommodate his well-developed belly. Dinners were timely and predictable—Shake & Bake chicken on Tuesday, tuna casserole on Wednesday, and meatloaf on Thursday. He would eat dinner at their Formica-top kitchen table and then savor his Tastykake Krumpets while sitting back on the pea-colored Strata Lounger in the den completely mesmerized by "Fantasy Island" and "Starsky & Hutch" on TV, his favorite shows to watch after working at the mill. Artie loved TV, and the actors on his shows. And what he loved even more was going to shows in Atlantic City to see people on TV live and in person.

On Friday nights, from the week after Easter until the week after the Miss America Pageant in September, Mrs. Winters did not have to make dinner for her son. During those months, every Friday at 6:10 Artie took the Greyhound bus from Philadelphia to the Atlantic City Bus Terminal on Arkansas Avenue—rain or shine. He would check his black Naugahyde bag into the luggage compartment in the belly of the bus. But his camera bag sat on his lap the entire ride, never leaving his sight.

It contained Artie's most precious possession, a large

format press camera with an attached bulb flash. He'd place the camera bag strap across his left shoulder and then another bag with film and lenses across his right shoulder crisscrossing his flabby belly.

To me, the black and silver contraptions resembled cameras you would see on an old "Perry Mason" episode where the press flashes away as Raymond Burr, playing Perry, talked about his current client that was in big trouble, looking very guilty, until Perry would figure out how to prove his innocence.

Artie loved taking pictures in Atlantic City. Saturday mornings could not arrive fast enough for him to walk the four blocks from St. James Place to Virginia Avenue on the Boardwalk, and spend the day taking pictures on Steel Pier.

As soon as the bus pulled into the terminal, Artie rushed to retrieve his bag, and then hailed a cab straight to St. James Place. As he paid the cabbie, he'd yell from the street up to the Seacrest Hotel, "Hello, Harry. Hello Missus, I'm here!"

My father, who usually sat at the front desk awaiting the next customer, would hear him and get Artie's key and guest registration card out—Artie liked knowing that someone was expecting him. He'd barrel into the lobby and my mother would immediately greet him with a tall glass of iced tea infused with her homemade strawberry preserves.

"Welcome back, Artie. Did you have a good week?" my mother would always ask. Her nearly five-foot-tall frame looked so small next to Artie.

"Oh yes, Missus! But I couldn't wait to come back and see you and Harry." Artie would clearly enunciate his words while attempting to tuck in his shirt tail that never stayed in place.

Artie sure looked forward to coming to the Seacrest on Friday night after his work week at the paper factory. He also spent his one vacation week a year at the Seacrest, ogling *Playboy* on the mustard-yellow chenille bedspread with a kitten embroidered into the middle of it. Artie liked that addition to his room.

Every Friday morning, my mother prepared Room 17 for him. He never suspected that the room was rented out during the week to other guests and my parents never gave him any reason for suspicion. Whether Artie was in attendance or not, my parents always referred to Room 17 as Artie's room. It was small, with a single bed, but it did have a private bath. My mother never forgot to change the bedspread and place his favorite stuffed elephant on the nightstand by the bed.

On rare occasions when my mother forgot to put the elephant in the room, Artie would immediately notice, yelling, "Missus, where's Dumbo?" My mother would fetch it from the linen closet, assuring him that she placed it there for safe keeping. With Dumbo back in its place,

Artie would calm down and brush back his poker-straight blondish bangs that fell on his face. He'd hug my mother and she would wish him sweet dreams, shutting the door and heading off to take care of another guest who needed towels.

My mother was never quite sure why a 32-year-old man needed a stuffed animal, but she accommodated his quirky needs—it made him happy. One weekend Artie caught a cold and could not come to the shore. His mother called to cancel his reservation and I overheard my mother talking to Mrs. Winters. I knew they were talking about Artie, but another person overhearing would have thought the two mothers were talking about a little boy.

"Yes, Vick's will be good to rub on his chest—and give him tea with lots of honey."

My mother's solution to all ailments was tea and honey. If things got serious, she had a powerful backup plan in the form of chicken soup. The two mothers exchanged recipes and some niceties, and my mother was off to make up Artie's room for another guest.

Artie liked telling my father all about who was headlining at Steel Pier that weekend. He'd ask my father if he liked Steve Lawrence or Paul Anka. My father, who never set foot on Steel Pier even after living three blocks away for over 15 years, would express an *oy vey* and randomly pick one of the names that Artie offered up to him—always smiling at his *meshuganeh* stories.

Artie would ask my father to come with him so he could give him a tour of the 2,000 foot pier jutting out over the ocean that entertained and amused people since the late 1800s—two movie houses showing feature films, the diving horse plunging into the Atlantic, the round and flimsy diving bell that submerged young and old into the murky waters at the end of the pier, and live shows starring the latest and the greatest, ranging from Al Jolson in the 1930s, to Frank Sinatra in the 1940s, to rock and pop stars like The Supremes and The Rolling Stones in its later years.

Every week there was a new headliner, and for 50 cents each in the late 60s, my friends and I would spend the day, especially a rainy one, watching *Butch Cassidy and the Sundance Kid* and bouncing to the top tunes performed by The Turtles or Herman's Hermits. By the time I was in high school, the Pier had lost its appeal, and the gambling referendum passed in 1976 was a final nail in its coffin.

No matter how many times Artie asked to take him to Steel Pier, my father would politely reply, "Maybe next time." But for a man who never left the front desk of the Seacrest from Memorial Day to Labor Day, it was an empty promise. Guests had to be checked in and out, supplies and linens ordered, beds made, the telephone in the booth had to be answered, and on a rare occasion, maybe a nap.

To my father's dismay, the conversation would continue and Artie would then ask, "Harry, who do you like better Bobbie Rydell or Sammy Davis?"

Once or twice during the summer season, Artie would bring his pal, Harvey, a tiny wisp of a man who looked twice as old as Artie. They seemed to be friends, but it was never quite clear to me how they met or why they were friends. Harvey always wore the same old, too big black suit that smelled of urine dribbles. His wrinkled face sported rough white whiskers that put a catfish to shame. Harvey didn't say much and hid behind Artie's bulky frame all weekend, occasionally grumbling and mumbling through his toothless mouth about how much Artie talked.

Harvey stayed in Room 15, one room away from Artie. In the morning, the pair would meet in the lobby and plan their day at Steel Pier. They loved watching the lady riding the horse as it plunged, but both enjoyed the *Tony Grant's Stars of Tomorrow* even more—mostly the pubescent little girls in sequin costumes and patent leather tap shoes performing on stage every two hours. For 32 years, Tony Grant, dapper and fatherly, emceed the show that gave thousands of kids an opportunity to strut their stuff in front of a live audience. Most would tap dance, pantomime, or sing mediocrely, at best, to the delight of their over eager stage moms or paid to persevere dance teachers. Every once and a while, a kid would wow the audience like an up and coming Frankie Avalon or a Connie Francis. Every show started with the Tony Grant theme song, "We're the Stars of Tomorrow Today. . ."—a catchy tune with simple rhyme and a 1930s Vaudeville beat.

In between Steel Pier shows, Artie would insist on lunch. The two would trot off one block away from the pier on the Boardwalk to the Taylor Pork Roll stand for a sandwich and a Coke. Artie's cumbersome belly and camera bags flapped up and down with each step, but it did not slow him down—a step and half behind lagged Harvey trying to keep up with his hungry buddy.

After a long day at Steel Pier, Artie would bring his photo albums down to the lobby or out on the large front porch in the evenings. He would sit on one of the rocking chairs lined up along the edge of the porch enjoying the ocean breeze while going through the pages of his precious albums.

"Artie, can I see your pictures again," I would ask if I was in the mood to see his black & white glossy treasures. He'd eagerly click the snap of the case and take out his prize, handling it like it was a newborn baby—gentle and cautiously. Other than looking at his photos, Artie and I rarely spoke. He was more comfortable chatting with my parents, and as a young teenager, that suited me just fine unless I wanted to see his famous people pictures.

Encased in plastic envelopes to keep each shot safe and preserved, each of the 20 pages in the album displayed four photos. Almost all the shots were Steel Pier performers taken from Artie's front row seat in the theater, but there was always a more personal photo with different people in the same pose—Artie on the left, with his large right arm around Peggy Lee, Bobby Vinton, Cab Calloway, or whoever was the star of the week.

Every September, the first week after Labor Day, Art was armed and ready with plenty of flash bulbs and film for the Miss America Pageant. He booked front row seats in advance at Convention Hall—especially the night of the swimsuit competition to make sure he had plenty of shots of his favorite contestant, usually Miss Pennsylvania.

Since its inception in 1921 as a "bathing beauty revue," the parading girls on stage from every state helped to elongate the summer season an extra week for Boardwalk merchants and to the zoom lens of Art's camera.

For some reason, I never bothered to ask Artie how he managed to seize these hundreds of photo opportunities on Steel Pier. But he always got perfect poses, everyone in the picture, especially Artie, frozen in time forever smiling and happy. And Artie, his white shirt tails never quite tucked into his pants and there was always a few strands of his straight blond hair out of place.

Chapter Three

Jimmy

Jimmy hadn't left the Johnstown, Pennsylvania area his whole life. His father couldn't really afford to help him get an education on his steel factory salary, and didn't really value a college degree anyway. Jimmy, who easily flew through school, decided to put himself through college by waiting tables during the summer in Atlantic City. When he was 17, he started saving money from odd jobs he did around town for a one-way Trailways bus ticket that he used the day after graduating from high school.

We hit it off right away. Jimmy was four years older, but we still hung out together. He knew no one in town and my school friends were in sleepy and safe Ventnor and Margate. So, he and I would go for walks on the Boardwalk or grab a piece of pizza from a tiny joint two blocks from the hotel—Napoli's, thin crust, basic, and cheap—perfect for our 14 and 18-year-old budgets.

One night, Jimmy and I walked the three blocks from the Seacrest to Pennsylvania Avenue to see the *Poseidon Adventure* at the Strand Theater—it was a hot movie to see that summer and ended up winning several Academy Awards. In 1972 the visual effects of a sinking cruise ship would not hold a candle to a Pixar extravaganza today, but Jimmy and I crouched down low in our seats when that rogue wave hit the cruise ship and the drownings began. As a result, poor Mrs. Rosen from New York City, played by Shelly Winters, would not make it to Israel and never meet her first grandchild—but Winters would go on to win Best Supporting Actress.

If you stood in front of the Strand Theater, located across the Boardwalk from Steel Pier, a unique aroma blend treated your senses. Popcorn smells from the theater wafted out to the Boardwalk and mixed with the sweet smells from the Belgium Waffle stand next door and the gamey, very *traif* Taylor Pork Roll stand next to that. If the breeze was blowing south, Planter's Peanut scents from 3-doors down would mingle into the air as well.

At the time, I never thought the smells and old Atlantic City skyline would disappear to make way for gambling giants, like Trump's failure of a monstrosity, the Taj Mahal. After the Gambling Referendum passed in New Jersey in 1976, not a single movie theater was left standing in Atlantic City—bull-dozed down to become gambling related businesses or empty lots that never were developed. All those sweet smells of cotton candy, fudge being formed on marble slabs right before your eyes, and Mr. Peanut waiving to kids in front of the store, faded away into nothing but scenes on vintage post cards of Atlantic City.

My father took to Jimmy immediately and thought he was a nice boy—*a finer ingle*. When he first moved into the hotel, he would spend his spare time watching TV in the lobby and talking to my father. They would discuss his earnings and calculate how much was needed towards meeting his goal for tuition in September.

"Harry, you're the first Jewish person I ever met. You have to teach me some Jewish," Jimmy asked.

Yiddish was my parents' native tongue and the unique, primary language for millions of Eastern European Jews.

My father happily indulged Jimmy with a lesson or two when he had some downtime sitting in the lobby waiting for the next customer.

First, he taught him to say, "Work was hard today, but I made lots of money." He memorized the phrase and would parrot it back to my father when he came home from work every day. I think my father was amused by Jimmy's unusually bad Yiddish as he awkwardly announced, *"Arbeit iz geven she-ver, obber ick hob gemackt goot!"*

Jimmy worked at a restaurant on New York Avenue, one street over from the Seacrest—another orange property on the Monopoly board. The street was known as the "gay" street in Atlantic City—lots of hot clubs like the Chez and Mama Mott's Italian restaurant. From the Boardwalk down to Pacific Avenue, it was a Mardi Gras, a party 24/7.

In the 1920s, when all of Atlantic City, in the aftermath of Prohibition, became a place of open booze and all manner of vice, Louise Mack opened a place called the Entertainer's Club, that catered, secretly, to homosexual men. Louise would decide, by your appearance, if you could enter. If so, you paid at the door and she stuffed many an entrance fee into her bra.

By 1964, the courts determined that homosexuals were not "undesirables" and the street exploded with drag shows, bars, hotels—a lifeline for gay men mostly—and one bar catering to women. Today, the street is barren and abandoned. Grindr and other hook up apps took the place of buying someone a drink at the Brass Rail or a tryst at the Lark Inn.

Although Jimmy wasn't gay in my observations, he told me that he didn't mind the "oh, I am so interested" looks from his customers. He just smiled and collected his much-needed tips. After a while, two men from North Jersey who frequented the restaurant befriended him. I never met them officially, but I saw them pull up to the Seacrest several times in their fancy Porche 911 convertible, top down, to whisk him away. I think their names were Barry and Lance, Lance may have been the blonde one who never wore a shirt.

Barry and Lance, slick and rich, seemed to feed off of Jimmy's fresh smile and the fact that he didn't know how to not trust another human being. Jimmy started spending less time in the lobby with my father and more time with his new friends who gave him expensive presents—new clothes and long evenings that led into mornings.

One night, Jimmy staggered into the lobby reciting the only line of Yiddish that he knew. *"Arbeit is ga-ven sha-ver oober ick gemaackt good,"* he managed to slur, mangling the sentence.

"Jimmy is *shikker*," my father sighed as he reached for the passkey hidden in an old cigar box behind the front desk. He pointed towards Jimmy's swaying body and said to me. "Go, take him upstairs. He's drunk—don't let him fall down."

Even though he was taller than me, I grabbed Jimmy and wrapped his arms over my shoulders in attempt to hold him up as we headed upstairs. "Come on, let's get you to your room." He smiled, and like an obedient Gumby let me lead him up the stairs. I was a bit annoyed at my father for giving his 14-year-old daughter this assignment. But as we started up the stairs, I felt glad that I could help my father get the *shikker* out of the lobby.

Unfortunately for me, Jimmy's room was on the 4th floor of the hotel. It seemed to work out at first, but his slow-motion movements and exaggerated steps made the trip to Room 47 seem like an eternity—16 steps to each floor, separated by a small landing every eighth step where Jimmy would smile, stop, and mumble to me or nobody in particular.

A few times he almost fell, but the gloss-white balusters, layered by seven decades of paint jobs, prevented Jimmy from tumbling twice. I did my best to keep him upright. Each floor had a different carpet swirl—Jimmy's was large green ferns, faded from foot-traffic, especially in front of the 4th floor's shared bathroom next to Jimmy's room. Finally, I let him into his room leaving the pass-key with the large green fob dangling in the door. Anxious to leave, I was about to turn around and exit when Jimmy started tracing each pink rose on the wallpaper with his finger. He gazed at the flora as if it was the first time he had ever witnessed such natural beauty in the faded wallpaper with an oblong tea colored stain from last year's Nor'easter.

Once he lost interest in touching and tracing the roses on the wall, he focused on things on his dresser. He picked up a container of baby powder, put it up to his lips, and thought he could drink from it as if it were a glass.

"Cut it out, Jimmy" I kept telling him. "Put that down, No, you can't drink baby powder!" I finally convinced him to go to bed. As I quietly closed the door behind me, I heard him softly giggling and talking to himself—non-sensical, at least to me. Walking back down to the lobby, I considered what to tell my father. Maybe Jimmy had consumed more than a just a few too many beers, but he was clearly on something else. Probably acid since he behaved like the people in Nancy Reagan's "Just Say No" to drugs campaign videos they showed us in Health Class.

When I got back to the lobby. I reported to my father that Jimmy was still *shikker*, but just fine. I decided not to detail what substances Jimmy had taken and didn't even know how to begin to explain acid trips to my father.

By mid- August, Jimmy's time in the lobby chatting with my father was very rare. He worked his shift, and immediately went out partying with his friends—many nights not coming home at all. Once in a while, Jimmy would take the time to assure my father that he was making enough money.

"I already have more than enough saved for college, Harry. I am good. Real good," he stated emphatically.

Although Jimmy appeared happy frequenting New York Avenue bars and clubs, his ghost-like skin color gave him a sickly appearance. His large brown eyes lost their innocence. When he would stagger in from a night out, my parents would remark about Jimmy and what had become of him, "*Oy, vos ken mir tonne far hem –a shanda –a shikker!*"

The innocent kid they checked into Room 47 three months ago was different, and it wasn't alcohol that was to blame. My mother considered calling his family, but wasn't sure what to say since she and my father weren't really sure what was going on. My father said to her one night while we were having dinner in the kitchen behind the front-desk that if they had to call each family member about a Seacrest guest's behavior, they would be on the phone all day and night. My father was right on target.

My mother did try to call Jimmy's family. She retrieved the army-green metal registration card box tucked under the front desk, and found Jimmy's card. He listed his Pennsylvania phone number, and my mother went into the phone booth in the lobby. She closed the door behind her, and the loud fan above her started whizzing. I heard coins clanging as she deposited money to make the call. She introduced herself to the woman who answered the call and tried to explain that she thought Jimmy needed his parents because he was hanging around with some "bad boys." I couldn't hear what she said back to my mother, but when my mother hung up the phone, she mumbled what a stupid cow, *"bahayma,"* for not caring enough to check up on her son.

She looked at me sitting on the sofa in the lobby and said, *"A meshugnaeh velt!"* There was no arguing with her that it was a crazy world at the Seacrest Hotel.

Then one morning in late August—perhaps it was inevitable—an Atlantic City police detective came to search his room at the Seacrest. He told my father that Jimmy jumped or fell off the roof of the Deauville Hotel, about one mile away from his rose-patterned room at the Seacrest. The case was under investigation.

"Ay, yai, yai," my father kept saying out loud, even

after the police left the hotel. My mother, on her way up to get the room ready for the next customer, sighed as she went up the stairs. I went with her and took the old sheets off the bed – the roses on the wallpaper seemed to look even more faded and washed out since I was last in Jimmy's room.

That night, my mother treated us with her noodle casserole. My father and I loved her *kugel*—crust fried on the outside to a golden brown, and salty with lots of oil-fried onions inside that made the Seacrest smell like our home until the ocean breeze wafted the aroma away. We didn't say much to each other as we ate.

Arbeit is geven shver, ober Ich hob gemacht goot.

Chapter Four

Natalie

In the dreary days of early May, Atlantic City would busily prepare itself for the upcoming summer season, which officially commenced on Memorial Day weekend. Store keepers would stock up on their supply of souvenir T-shirts and Salt Water Taffy boxes stacked in neat, orderly columns; lots of details to take care of before the summer started. On the amusement piers, mechanics on Central and Million Dollar Pier busily tested the rides; oiling and painting everything from the red and yellow Tilt-a-Whirl cups to the multi-colored Ferris Wheel spokes. Once Memorial Day weekend arrived, the city would be ready to feed, house, and amuse day trippers coming to the city for a few hours or its summer-long guests, all splashing on the beach by day and walking the Boardwalk by night.

By the last weekend in May, the city would be ready to open her doors and make most of her anticipated annual income in the next 10 weeks of summer.

At the Seacrest, my mother would oversee the annual Spring cleaning of the rooms and lobby. Mattresses were turned over and cleaned, carpets shampooed, and all the blinds tested to make sure they would roll up once a guest pulled on the dingy tassel dangling from the bottom of the blinds. They were always functional, but smelled like a plastic cup left on the heat of a stove mixed in with a dash of salty sweat. My father would concentrate on supplies—making sure there was enough toilet paper, cleaning materials, and finalizing contracts with the laundry supplier who faithfully delivered clean sheets and towels sealed in cellophane wrappers twice a week during the summer.

It was the weekend before Memorial Day, and I was with my parents at the hotel because they were too busy to go back and forth to Ventnor. In a few weeks, I would be graduating from 8th grade and spending the entire summer at the Seacrest before starting Atlantic City High School in September. Race riots were exploding across the country in 1971, and Atlantic City was no exception. Neighborhoods were quite segregated until the late 60s—Italians occupied 2-3 square blocks called Ducktown in the center of the city. Adjoining the Italian neighborhood was a smaller block or two with Irish. Jews lived primarily in the inlet section—the top end of the island. Black families were on the North side—furthest away from the beach and Boardwalk. Kids with older brothers and sisters warned us that there would be cafeteria fights and maybe a fist-fight between black boys from the North side of Atlantic City and white boys from neighboring and very sheltered Margate. By the time school started, tensions were on a simmer. Only one large fight broke out during my freshman year; a cafeteria food fight. No one was hurt and classes would resume without any fanfare the following day.

To help with the prepping, I volunteered to organize the linen closet on the second floor—always padlocked and lined with sheets and towels for the hotel. I had a small transistor radio with me and apropos to the day's weather, The Carpenters were singing about rainy days and Mondays always getting them down as the rain continued to fall. Once I completed my task, I headed back to the lobby to catch the end of a Phillies game on the TV just in time to see them beat the Mets 4-1. Unfortunately, for Philadelphia and her fans, the team would finish in last place for the National League East that year.

The tap tap of the rain was constant all day and the faux grass carpet on the steps up to the Seacrest porch squished with each step that Natalie Wilson took on her way up to the lobby. She seemed pretty under those sad eyes, but that afternoon her hair was wet and stringy from walking in the rain looking for a reasonable and safe place to stay. I saw her leave the neighboring Seabreeze Hotel—sister to the Seacrest in structure and built in 1912, but more wholesome and family oriented. The owner, cantankerous and bigoted Mr. O'Malley, barely acknowledged my parents since my father was not drinking buddy material for him. There was an attitude about him that I could smell a mile away—dirty Jews, niggers, and faggots. Nope, none of that in his fine establishment. Natalie may have been blonde and fair skinned, but she had no money.

Natalie walked up to the lacquered front desk to ask my father about a room, her face and arms tattooed from recent bruises an angry husband somewhere in Ohio gave her. Without a single word my Father knew the story. The black and blue marks exposed her last eight years: going from her parent's home right out of high school, to a drunk of a husband who would not entertain her working, going back to school, or having any friends.

Natalie hid a few dollars each week from the allowance her husband gave her until she saved up for a Greyhound ticket. She decided to go to Atlantic City because she never saw the beach and as a little girl and loved watching the Miss America pageant on television every September. Once she figured out a plan to leave the house, Natalie took only a small suit case and headed to the bus station downtown leaving her small rambler—door unlocked and mail box flap open.

My father took to Natalie right away. She seemed nice and, more importantly to my father, quiet. He showed her a couple of rooms and told her the prices—per week to be paid in advance. She confessed up front that she had no money to pay for a room. She dried her wet hands on the lining of her rain coat, and took off her tiny engagement ring that at this moment meant nothing more than a glittering barter tool. She asked my father to keep the ring for collateral until she could make some money and pay for her room in cash. It was a small diamond ring, not worth very much, but my father couldn't say no to the lady with bruises on her arms and an almost healed yellowish patch under her eye. He let her "borrow" on it and she lived in Room 27 until all the bruises healed.

He had her fill out the Seacrest guest registration card at the front desk—name, address, and make of car. She probably did not write her real address, but my father would say she was from Ohio whenever he spoke about her to my mother. He gave her the key to a small room, on the second floor, but got the afternoon light to brighten the blue and gray plaid bedspread. Natalie teared up as she walked up to her new room clutching the Seacrest Hotel key with the oval green fob—*if lost, drop in any US Postal mail box...We guarantee postage.*

My mother looked at my father and told him that he did the right thing letting the poor girl stay and try to get her life in order, *"A rachmonas. A shayne maydel."* They felt sorry for her—maybe being kicked about and thrown out during the war instilled empathy in them? Maybe they were just born with the gene? Maybe it was a hybrid—in any case, Natalie had a safe place to stay.

After a few days, she found a job on the Boardwalk as a counter girl at the Belgium Waffle shop. Her boss, a huge man with a bellowing voice, would hock his sugary wares by yelling out over the Boardwalk attracting customers a block away as she served the doughy delights.

"Get your tasty Belgium Waffles—come on up and ohhhhhhh, they smell sooooo good."

Natalie would come back to her room each night apron covered with powdered sugar, smelling of vanilla extract and the echo of the Belgium Waffle *shtick* in her ears. She eventually started to smile more and talk a little to my parents and other hotel guests she met in the lobby.

Towards the end of July, an Atlantic City police officer, whose beat included the Waffle shop right across from Steel Pier, would walk Natalie back to the Seacrest after her shift ended at night. At first, he would wait for her in the lobby to change out of her confectioner's sugar-coated uniform and then go out with him for a walk or a drink. He was very quiet and stern. I thought it was because he was a cop, but I overheard Natalie telling my mother that he was married and their relationship was not "kosher" as my mother would later explain to my father.

Natalie clearly lit up when her police officer was around her—the miles of disappointment etched into her face when she first moved into the Seacrest were fading away. On some occasions, he would walk her home and whenever possible, spend the night with her. I found out his first name was Donald because I would overhear her say his name when they were making love in Room 27.

On weekdays, if rooms were vacant, I could pick any room in the hotel to sleep in, sometimes it was a random choice and other times calculated—wanting to wake up with a certain view of the beach, or in Natalie's case, walking very slowly back and forth past her door catching the gutter groans coming from the room. On many nights, Natalie would leave the transom open and I could hear their whispered conversations. He would tell her, softly, that "I just can't get enough of you." After walking, quietly and oh so deliberately, past her room a few times my curiosity was complete. Maybe I sensed that eavesdropping, even if my reasons for being in the hallway could pass for innocent, was not right. I went to my room, and left them to their whispers.

Officially learning about the "birds and bees" was covered in health class when I was 12, complete with a Disney animation movie—one for the boys and another for the girls. Shortly after I had had the sex education class, my mother nervously tried to bring up the subject. I pulled out my little pink booklet with cheery illustrations of fallopian tubes and sanitary napkin products and told her we already learned about it in school. She quickly flipped through the booklet. Convinced they were covering all the angles, she gave the booklet back to me and sighed in relief, "Oh, thank goodness…"

About four years before the little pink booklet and the moans coming out of Natalie's room, I decided to hide under the bed in Room 34 while my mother changed the linens. There was a Bic pen, a crumpled Kleenex, and a wrinkled copy of a Playboy magazine with the centerfold already opened half way. I opened the magazine and saw a girl who looked like a beautiful fairy princess, light diffused all around her as she lay on a bed with sheer curtains blowing across her pretty much naked body.

Besides her puckered red lips, what got my attention were her breasts, almost round and full like they could pop any minute. I knew this was not something I should be looking at since I was not even 9, but kept leafing through the pages anyway. It was fun to be doing something that must be bad and not getting caught. But, at the same time, looking at nothing but naked princesses just got a little boring and I started to read a short story that was in the issue. It seemed too long of a reading commitment to finish under the bed, so I tore out the pages and decided to read it later.

I did not get most of the story. It had nothing to do with naked ladies. It had everything to do with a psychiatrist who could not take hearing the complaints of his patients another day—frivolous, self-absorbed, and trivial. Then, a new patient arrives claiming to be God—THE one and only God—and that he needs someone to talk to because of the stress and burdens that he carries on his shoulders. The psychiatrist thinks he is just another nut. When God senses this, he gets fed up with the psychiatrist and all of whining humanity and decides to end the world that night. God warns the psychiatrist that when he hears the bathroom faucet drip that night, it will be over after the third drip.

The fed-up psychiatrist goes home, pours himself a few drinks, talks about changing careers, and then the story ends with ".... then he heard the faucet drip—once, twice, and then a third time."

I have tried to find the story again when I was a little older to re-read it. No idea what the title was or who wrote it. I also had no clue what I was reading, it was clearly for an older reader. But, I never forgot that story and wondered if God would ever need to talk to someone about his problems.

Natalie moved out a few weeks after Labor Day weekend. Donald rented an apartment for her and was divorcing his wife so they could get married. When my father tried to give back her engagement ring, she closed his hand around the tiny piece of metal and thanked him for letting her stay at the Seacrest.

"Harry, I don't want that ring. You let me stay here before I had a job or money. It's not even real gold, and you trusted me." She gave my father a hug good bye.

He wished her well and said, "You're a good girl. Good luck to you.

My mother asked her to wait a minute. She ran back into the kitchen and insisted that Natalie take a bag of her *mandel broit* cookies, my mother's signature treat. She hugged my mother and walked out of the lobby with Donald carrying the small suitcase she brought with her from Ohio.

For years, I would notice the cheap ring in the back of my mother's jewelry box. When I asked her why she kept it, she did not have an answer. "I don't know why—probably something from the hotel. One day I'll put it in the trash."

Chapter Five

Lolly & Me

Even though the Traymore Hotel was four blocks away from the Seacrest, the earth rumbled and the windows in my room rattled like a California earthquake when the grand building was imploded in 1972. I was 15 years old, and this was a big deal for me to watch from my perch at the Seacrest, and for the city to endure. After the noise, there was silence as a fog of whitish gray dust wafted away from where 60 years of proper clientele once wined and dined overlooking the Boardwalk.

It was surreal to watch 400 rooms filled with once-upon-a-time elegance, like bathtubs offering hot and cold ocean water, crumble into a pile of powder and debris within seconds.

In the 1920s, the hotel was dubbed the "Taj Mahal of

Atlantic City," decades before Donald Trump opened a casino by the same name, but without an ounce of the Traymore's style or class. In the late 60s, the Traymore and Atlantic City in general began deteriorating. Airplanes and long-distance traveling were not just for the rich and the famous. As a result, vacations to Disney and Las Vegas became more affordable and accessible. Atlantic City found herself losing her world famous appeal—finding herself like the cliché older wife replaced by the glitzy young secretary.

Eight years after the implosion, film director Louie Malle used actual footage of the implosion as an artistic symbol representing the city's decline and literal downfall in his classic film, *Atlantic City*. Much of the movie was filmed in and around the city—complete with Susan Sarandon cleansing her young body with lemons after working in the Oyster Bar at Resorts International, the first casino to open its doors in Atlantic City in 1978.

At the time, legal, state-sanctioned gambling was supposed to be the silver bullet that would save the city. Bookies and number runners, be damned! Unfortunately, 12 casinos and 40 years later, gambling revenues never quite revived the town thanks to political mischief and the mishandling of funds and trusts including two mayors who went to jail, and a third well on his way. So, the movie tells the story of two lost people falling apart who needed help—an allegory for the decline in Atlantic City.

Enter Stage Left - craggy, old Burt Lancaster mustering up his gangster juju to help a damsel in distress.

During the filming of the movie in 1979, I was working at Resorts International during summer and winter breaks while I was in my last year of college. My auspicious job title, Safety Deposit Box Clerk, put me in the Assistant Manager's/Security office where anything from a lost child, to prostitutes at the bars, to extra towel requests would come through. One night, my manager asked me to take flowers delivered for Burt Lancaster up to his suite. I knocked on his door expecting an assistant or someone other than the actor himself. To my surprise, he answered the door in boxer shorts and wife beater T-shirt, took the flowers, and did not tip me for my efforts.

When the movie was released in 1980, watching "Atlantic City" in a movie theater in Atlantic City surrounded by locals, some who were extras in the film, felt like being in a movie about a movie. You could hear people whispering about streets and scenes they recognized. When I saw Burt Lancaster in his underwear on the big screen, I laughed to myself remembering the same outfit when I delivered his flowers.

The only time I actually set foot in the Traymore Hotel was in 1972, a few weeks before the demolition. They held a liquidation sale, and they were serious. Everything in the hotel was offered to the public. From no longer shiny chrome, standing ashtrays with dark amber glass, to Nippon blue china tea cups and saucers used to serve high tea—buy it now or it becomes rubble.

One of my best friends was Lolly. Yes, Lolly and Molly, and much to our chagrin people would tease us with, "Is there a Polly?" I met Lolly in fourth grade when I moved from the farm in Vineland to Atlantic City. I started in the middle of the school year at Richmond Avenue School in the Chelsea section of Atlantic City—a bit more residential than the more tourist-centric area of the city.

Mrs. Hartman, my new teacher who had the tightest and most elegant French twist of silver hair, introduced me to the 4th grade class. I was nervous. She put her hands on my shoulder, told the class my name, and said, "I am going to sit you next to Sue Mickles." Sue smiled at me with big brown eyes that had a twinkle of mischief. We became friends instantly and were always at each other's houses. To this day, Sue reminds me that my mother's French toast was the best she ever ate.

At recess, I met Lolly, Lisa, Jill, and a few other girls from the neighborhood. Although I initially missed my life on the farm, I felt better knowing I had made new friends to play with, go on the beach, take a jitney up to Steel Pier, or walk to Lambert's ice cream parlor for a milkshake. Through many more years together of school, crushes, college, marriages, children, and divorces, the Richmond Avenue girls that I met years ago are still among my closest friends. In fact, not a day goes by that

Lolly and I don't get together or at the very least, chat on the phone about family, politics, and "what's wrong with people," our general, catch all topic.

As we walked up the Boardwalk to the Traymore Hotel, Lolly and I were determined to grab a souvenir or two, without any real idea what our teenage budget would permit. Neither one of us had ever been inside the grand hotel, so we knew it was now before demolishing day or never. There was nothing in particular that I wanted to buy, just window shopping. We made it a day by walking up the Boardwalk, snooping around, and say good bye to the Traymore.

When we entered the lobby, the old-time elegance now looked more like a flea market. Tables were set up everywhere with miscellaneous hotel and restaurant items piled here and there. An entire table scattered with clear glass ashtrays. Another set of tables stacked heavy, cream colored dishes from the coffee shop—some with stains impossible to wash off. In a meeting room off the lobby, stacks of rolled up rugs were leaned against the wall arranged by size, smaller ones on the left and larger to the far right. One rug laid flat on the floor—Oriental royal blue with a border of ornate birds boasting long feather tails. Amid all the stuff, we noticed clothes racks lined with bellman's jackets, complete with shoulder epaulets and the Traymore Hotel embroidered in gold on the breast pocket.

Lolly stopped and pointed, "Look at those jackets. How cool...like a Sgt. Pepper's jacket."

We tried on jackets until we found just the right fit. She got the Captain's jacket, a little baggy, but in our minds the cool factor was worth it. I got a regular bellman's jacket sans the epaulets but pretty nifty with gold braided tubing down the arms. All we could think of was how cool we would be with our worn-out bell bottom jeans and oversized Traymore bellboy jackets.

Lolly lived a few miles away from the Seacrest Hotel in Ventnor, a quiet and clean-as-a-whistle town where day-tripper tourists seldom visited and pimps and prostitutes would never dare. As a yearly treat, Lolly's mom would let her sleep over at the Seacrest one night during the summer. Since Lolly lived close to the end of the Atlantic City Jitney line, she just walked from her house and hopped a Jitney. Twenty-five cents and five minutes later, she pulled the buzzer on New York Avenue to tell the driver one stop prior that she wanted to get off on St. James Place.

After Lolly dropped off her overnight bag, we would immediately go up to the Boardwalk and walk six blocks to Million Dollar Pier, while debating if we would get homemade Italian Water ice or cannoli for dessert. Before we got on the rides at the front of the pier, we followed our noses to the back to the Italian Village, where you could always count on the unique smell coming from a mix of food vendors. Dozens of stalls offered scents like sweet-onions and hot peppers packed into plump sub sand-

wiches. Vendors sold hot and cold food. Some prepared
to eat and others deli style to take home. The smells of
large wheels of pecorino and parmesan next to vats of
mozzarella balls and olives, green and black, tantalized
the senses. And adding to the mix, huge garlicy salamis
hung in rows from deli meat vendors—another item that
I would not eat because they were forbidden in my parent's kosher home.

"Don't you bring home any of that *chazzerye*," my
mother would warn us about bringing home unkosher
food. What I could bring home was cannoli, sweet and
creamy, and kosher enough since it was just dairy. Instead
of water ice at the pier, we decided to get two cannoli,
wrapped in waxy paper and then carefully placed in a
white paper bag, to eat when we got back to the Seacrest.
For dinner, Lolly would get a slice of pizza speckled
with pepperoni. I got a plain piece, no meat. Although
my parents preferred that I not eat anywhere or anything
that came close to *traif*, they understood they had to adapt
their ways for me and eased their rules—just a tad as far
as I was concerned, but an enormous step and adjustment
for my parents and their Orthodox upbringing in Poland.
So, I was allowed to eat pizza as long as it did not have
meat on it. A deal I could live with.

After the pizza, we stopped to see the organ grinder
with its little monkey in striped pants that tipped his hat
if you gave him money. As we exited the back of the pier,

the smells of cheese and deli faded as the shrills of people laughing on the colorful and lit up rides took center stage. Although Million Dollar Pier still stands and jolts out over the Atlantic, its honky-tonk days have been long over. After several attempts at being a shopping mall, the pier currently awaits a new injection of money from yet another corporation attempting to make it vibrant once again. In the meantime, a few restaurants and shops exist touting gorgeous ocean views from any angle as you stroll through the enclosed once upon a time Million Dollar Pier.

After walking around a bit after our meal, Lolly and I bought tickets for several rides. The Haunted House was our favorite on Million Dollar Pier. A rickety 2-seater car that took you from the bright summer light into a dark and dingy world, on a moldy-smelling track that twisted through presumably gauze cob webs. Ghouls and zombie-like dummies, so obviously fake and stiff, would mechanically fall in front of the cars and then get retracted back as an automated recording screeched and howled at the exact same twist and turn on the 4-minute ride.

Then there was the Octopus—appropriately named for its tentacle-like steel arms that carried four in a car and would spin as the arms went up and down. If Alan was working the rides, he would let us sit up there for hours on slow nights—dangling over the crashing waves beneath the pier. Alan lived at the Seacrest in the summers. He told my father it was easy for him to find a job in Atlantic

City. I overheard my father telling my mother that Alan is a "*shtamlicker*,—someone who stuttered and sadly, was not very employable.

After Labor Day, Alan would go back to his mother's trailer home in Atco, NJ and drink away his unemployment checks. He was always very friendly to me, "Hey kid, here's a s-s-s-special ride for you and your f-f-ffriend." For the price of one ticket, he let Lolly and me stay on the ride over and over until Alan decided to let us off or the lines for other kids who wanted to get on the ride became too long.

When we were done with Million Dollar Pier, Lolly and I would also stop by the Atlantic City Bus Terminal, which was just a block down from the Boardwalk on Arkansas Avenue. Lolly's aunt worked there so we had a legitimate reason to stop by and say hello, but Lolly and I thought it was a hoot to just sit in the terminal and watch the characters coming and going, waiting to take the next bus to Camden, New York, and all the other destinations that New Jersey Transit could offer. The terminal, a classic building typical of 1930's architecture, was originally built as the train station for the Pennsylvania Reading Seashore Line—bringing tourists from Philadelphia into Atlantic City, was showing signs of aging after 40 years of use. In the early 90s, the building was demolished and a new bus station was built several blocks over. Today if you come and go through the new station, pieces of the old still exist.

Like the art deco chandelier layered in a chevron pattern hanging from the center ceiling and the ornate iron clock which still kept time perfectly.

We sat in the back row of the bus station sharing our comments and opinions about the bus people. The single stadium-like seats, intentionally hard and uncomfortable, discouraged bums who wanted to spend the night, as did security guards. Sometimes we would giggle out loud, Lolly's infectious laugh just made us laugh even more. People passing by never knew what we were laughing at—or so we hoped. "Look what just walked in the door. Can you believe that guy has his clothes on inside out," Lolly would remark. We'd exchange snickers and snarky comments until the next oddity disembarked a bus, many times inebriated, often haunted by demons.

On occasion, the sites could be more pleasant like catching a glimpse of Officer Bradley—a cute rookie for ACPD assigned to the bus terminal, 4-12 shift. He would wink at us with those deep brown eyes knowing damn well how handsome he was to any female—including Lolly and me. Even Bertha Johnson would notice his infectious eyes. She was a regular bus rider who used the terminal every day to get to and from her job where she kept house for a doctor in nearby Margate's "gold coast" neighborhood—stately and old money mansions near the beach.

When Officer Bradley was near, she would drop her worn out leather bag and announce, "My, my, my...that is a mighty fine lookin' boy—if I was a bit younger—oh my, my, my." She'd lick her cracked lips, pick up her bag with arthritic skelton-like hands, and slowly climb onto the bus heading to misnomer Pleasantville—a 10-minute ride west of Atlantic City to her one-bedroom bungalow with no air conditioning.

By the time Lolly and I got back to the hotel, the powder sugar and ricotta cheese from our cannoli had stained the bag, letting us know it was time for our Italian Village treat. My mother would follow us into the kitchen behind the front desk to give us white paper plates for the cannoli. Although my parents would occasionally eat dairy food at a restaurant, they preferred to eat home where my mother prepared her own meals—kosher and in my mother's Eastern European style that was usually packed with lots of onions fried in chicken *schmaltz* fat.

"Girls, you want some cold tea?" My mother wouldn't wait for an answer and pour us big glasses of her home-made iced tea made from Sweet-Touch-Nee bags that came in a red, tin container that always sat atop the stove.

We would offer her a bite of cannoli, but she'd wrinkle up her nose in disapproval and tell us, "No *chazzerye* from a store." Then she would bring out her home baked *mandel broit* cookies, sealed in a large glass jar; toasted golden brown with specks of walnuts, raisins, and occasionally some chocolate chips.

Chapter Six

Three Nice Boys In Apartment #1

The Seacrest consisted of 40 rooms. For an extra $5.00 a week, you could get one of the 10 rooms with private baths. All other rooms came with a small, free standing sink bolted to the wall offering hot and cold knobs; white porcelain, shaped like a pudgy X. At the end of each hallway was a full communal bathroom that all guests at the Seacrest were free to use.

On the street level, two narrow apartments stretched back the length of the hotel. The front rooms were small kitchenettes with a yellow Formica table top and metal chairs each from different sets, faced St. James Place— often benefitting from the ocean breeze. The back of the apartment, where two small bedrooms were located, was dark and plain, but always clean. My mother would have it no other way. If maintaining the Seacrest was billed as an Olympic event, there would be low scores for style and grace of the décor, but a solid 10 for cleanliness.

In the summer of 1976, the Bicentennial Year, three guys in their early 20s rented Apt # 1. My father called them, "nice college boyez." They told my mother that they had been friends since sixth grade and agreed to rent an apartment together at the beach in AC while working and partying—a great way to have fun and make some much needed money for college tuitions.

They were cute, at least in my 17-year old's assessment, like typical college students - which at the Seacrest made them stand out. Usually, most college kids preferred the down beach scene in Margate as opposed to the heart of Atlantic City. Located only five miles away, the clientele changed dramatically from the Seacrest to more residential and affluent Margate. Although most real estate was too expensive for students, Margate's back-bay area, off Amherst Avenue, had small, cottage beach houses. There, dozens of college kids rented for the summer. At night, a row of bars provided cheap beer and socialization along the bay at loud watering holes like `Memories featuring DJ Jerry Blavat – "The Geator with The Heator" spinning tunes where you could "Shake, Shake, *Shake Your Booty*" to K.C. and the Sunshine Band.

Dan and Jamie drove down together from Pittsburgh in late May, right before Memorial Day weekend, and moved into the apartment at the Seacrest. Ted, who trusted his friends' judgement, arrived on Memorial Day to join his pals for the season. As I watched them unload their cars and move into the apartment, I kept thinking to myself that these clean cut "college boys" did not seem to fit in with most of the other Seacrest guests.

My parents seemed to like them, and everyone was on a first name basis from the start. It's not that they hovered over the guys or anyone else in the hotel, but a guest knew, if they needed anything, my parents were there 24/7. Although the boys looked forward to a summer of being independent and away from home, having a mother figure around was comforting.

"Thanks, Sonia. You're the best," Dan told my mother when she brought them extra towels, sheets, and mini bars of ivory soap. Throughout the summer, I saw her give them little bags of her *mandel broit* cookies.

Dan and Jamie were active members in the Republican Party, and proudly wore their red, white, and blue Young Republicans t-shirts. On many occasions, they would talk about the ins and outs at their last convention. They met and mingled with Gerald Ford's younger children, Steven and Susan, who were about their ages. I was not old enough to vote at the time, but still enjoyed talking about politics. *Saturday Night Live* was on fire during the 1976 election year, Ford vs Carter. Whenever the guys talked about Ford all I could imagine was Chevy Chase's version of the bumbling incumbent President Ford telling his stuffed dog, Liberty, to roll over.

Dan was the better story teller, he would tell each story with a dash of drama. He would take his tortoise rimmed glasses on and off, depending on whatever character he was imitating. Blessed with a head of thick and straight hair, he could push it all back or tussle into a mess, as needed. Jaime, on the other hand, was quiet, maybe a bit shy, and his tall and lanky body would oversee his two friends, literally. He wore gold wire-frame glasses that matched his poker straight blonde hair with bangs always falling in front of his face. Jamie would push his bangs sideways to the right each time he corrected Dan's elaborate stories about who was chasing after who at the Republican Convention that year.

"Oh, what the hell does it matter, J?" Dan would roll his head and eyes and then smile from ear to ear, and resume spinning his tale the way he saw fit.

"Danny, you could never tell the truth—ever. Why are you always making shit up?" Jaimie would ask with a tone of annoyed superiority.

"Jamie, my good man, life is boring so let me embellish the truth a bit for emphasis!"

Ted, political leanings unknown to me since he did not display it with a T-shirt, was majoring in Criminology at Penn State. He planned to join the police force back home in Pittsburgh after graduation.While Dan and Jaime were tall and thin, Ted, on the other hand, was shorter and had no problem showing off his well-defined pecs and his great biceps; he looked somewhat like a chiseled Greek statue. Ted devoted many hours in the gym to improve his abilities to be able beat up bad guys one day.

Dan and I would sit on the porch and talk about stuff—mostly about the other Seacrest denizens and their secrets. As the landlord's daughter, I was privy to lots of info and Dan loved to chat and gossip about who was sleeping with whom. Like when he saw the guy in Room 30, who always wore platform shoes and lots of fake gold necklaces, sneak upstairs with two different girls the same night.

As the summer got rolling, we all worked Boardwalk and tourist jobs in town. With their wholesome good looks and clean-cut appearances, Jaimie and Dan made terrific tips parking cars for wealthy patrons out for a seafood dinner at the elegant Knife & Fork Inn. The restaurant, which has been in business since 1912 in Atlantic City, has served whatever needed to be served to the right people. From its inception as an exclusive drinking and dining club for men only to a Prohibition speakeasy that was protected by city boss Nucky Johnson (AKA Nucky Thomson from the HBO *Boardwalk Empire* series), the Knife and Fork, with its décor of crossed knives and forks on the exterior of the Tudor-like building, still is a draw today.

My summer job at Souvenir City on the Boardwalk

catered to the less upper-crust crowd. We sold 79 cent packs of Nudie Cards, 99 cent flip flops, T-shirts with decals including "Fireman Have Big Hoses" and "I'm With Stupid," and head supplies from bongs to roach clip necklaces.

Atlantic City, the consummate hostess, could and would entertain and please you no matter what your tastes were—you want it, you got it—contributing to her rises and falls since she became a beach resort in the late 1800s.

First scouted as a potential health resort in the mid 1850's, the incredible beaches of Southern New Jersey aways caught the eye of inspiring entrepreneurs. The first hotel, the Bellhouse, was built in 1853 and since then tourists and businessmen alike flocked the area. The first boardwalk was built in 1870 as a remedy to keep sand out of hotels but eventually came to serve tourists and shops.

One Friday night, Jaime and Ted were working at the parking lot jockeying cars. By coincidence, Dan and I both had the day off and we decided to go up on the Boardwalk and get a custard twist-cone from the Kohr Bros stand two blocks from the hotel. We took the long way back and meandered down New York Avenue, the gay street next to the Seacrest, where we saw lots of guys holding hands, kissing, and an occasional drag queen prancing down the street getting more than one wolf whistle. Half way up the block, we turned into an alley that cut over right to the Seacrest Hotel.

"So, do you like living right in the middle of fag alley?" Dan asked me as we settled into our favorite rockers on the Seacrest porch. He carefully looked at me with his big green eyes through his aviator glasses with intent.

"I spend all my summers here, and most of the customers are gay. So, I guess I don't even notice or care," I answered Dan never really giving it much thought.

During the winter, after the summer season and when school began, my family would go back to our house in Ventnor; a few miles away, but much more residential and much less sleazy. I almost never went to the hotel when I was in school. My father most of the time, or my mother, would take a Jitney bus that stopped on Jackson Avenue, right in front of our house, to the hotel two miles up Pacific Avenue to check on things for a few hours each day.

Off-season, my father let the "winter manager," Mac, run the place. Mac and his perpetually bloodshot eyes, from a continuous flow of cheap whiskey, conveyed when my parents bought the hotel in the early 70s. He ran the place like it was his own when he was on duty, usually not sober. My father tolerated him and his booze, but was not fond of him.

Drinking, more specifically over drinking, was not suitable for my father—especially at a bar. He would occasionally have a beer with a meal, and always a glass of Manischewitz kosher wine for Kiddush every Friday night.

Other than that, he felt a person who drinks in "saloons," his term for bar, is nothing but a *shikker* and a bum.

Pointing emphatically towards a gay couple turning into an alley from St James Place to cut over to New York Avenue Dan asked, "What do your parents think of all of this?"

"I don't think they care as long as you pay your rent and keep quiet!"

I then told Dan the story about the conversation I heard my mother have with her friend, Sylvia Schwartzman, about gay people. I overheard my mother listening to Sylvia prattle on about a mutual friend's daughter who was dating a black man. My mother, thanks to her life at the Seacrest seeing girls dating girls replied to Sylvia, "So, what. I don't care what color he is. At least he's a man." Dan howled with laughter. He could not imagine his Puritan-like mother understanding or even trying to understand homosexuality. And, then he decided the coast was clear.

"Just so you know. Jaime and I are gay. We aren't a couple or anything, but we came out to each other over a year ago."

Now I understood why these nice college boys didn't go to Margate and chase college girls. They preferred chasing boys, and that was much easier and more acceptable in Atlantic City.

"Oh, OK," my non-plus response since being gay

was no big deal to me after years of living in the hotel. I remember when I saw my first gay male—or at least looking back, I thought he was. Mr. Jonathon Jones from New York City. He was sitting in the lobby; a very shiny-skinned and soft-spoken man. What I remember the most was that he had the most beautiful hands for a man that I ever saw in my entire 8 years on earth; very clean, soft, and perfectly filed nails coated with clear polish.

From then on, Dan talked to me in a new way—more at ease, free to comment on any guy's butt that looked good to him. I guess telling me his "secret" allowed him to be the Dan he wanted to be as opposed to the Dan he was supposed to be.

I asked him about Ted. Ted looked like the last person on earth to be gay, but perhaps I misjudged. Dan assured me that he was straight and even more important, he did not know that Jaime and he were gay.

"We should tell him. Really. He's one of our oldest friends, but he would freak out if we told him. Mr. Macho would just freak out."

As the summer wore on, I also got to be friends with Ted—which was easy for a teenage girl to do. One hot August night, Jaime and Dan were working at the Knife, as they called it, and afterwards went cruising around the gay bars on New York Avenue—and did not invite Ted. I was sitting on the porch in jean cut off shorts, frayed of course, and a white T-shirt with the Ms. Magazine logo emblazoned on the chest. Ted came up from the apartment to the porch and found me there. We sat and talked for a while and then decided to walk the Boardwalk to see if we could catch more of the ocean breeze that was barely moving through the heavy air.

"Hey, why do you think Jaimie and Dan never ask me to go out with them? I ask them to come with me when I go to Margate, but it's like they don't want to hang out with me." Ted truly did not know what his childhood friends were doing and how they had changed.

"I guess you are on different schedules," I lied, hoping to make him feel better. We were leaning against the railing on the Boardwalk near Central Pier.

"You know, if it wasn't for you, I'd have just about nobody to talk to at the Seacrest." Ted leaned in to me and kissed me. Nice and sweet.

"I'll tell ya. If you weren't the landlord's daughter, I'd take you home tonight." We lived in the same place, but I clearly understood the subtle meaning of "home."

What I wanted to say is "what does that matter," but I just smiled, shyly, and we kept on walking and talking. When we got back to the hotel, Ted kissed me good night and thanked me for being a good friend. Not sure if he was putting the moves on me or just being nice to the landlord's daughter. I just let it go, nervous that I might say something about Dan and Jamie's sexual preferences.

I went upstairs wishing I was not related to the landlord, even just for a few hours, and decided that I would tell Dan in the morning that they had to tell Ted what was going on. It was not right.

For some reason, I could not find Dan in the morning and he and Jaime worked the following night as well. After Ted returned from his day job, security guard at the nearby Empress Motel, he joined me on the porch with a beer and lots of stories to tell about his day at work.

He really enjoyed talking about crime and police work, he was destined to become a cop. *Beshert* as it is said in Yiddish—kismet, pre-planned, what the universe intends it to be. First, he told me all about a robbery at the motel. The guy ran past his post and the cops from ACPD needed him to describe everything he had seen. Ted was almost giddy talking about it.

There were other guests on the porch, a few of Kennie's drag show friends, and a young couple just staying for the weekend. They were not paying any attention to Ted until he started talking about a magazine he found while on his security detail the other night at Convention Hall.

"So, this magazine was disgusting. All about gay guys and what they do to each other." Ted was shocked and amazed, in an almost innocent way, about the details.

"Did you know they stick their fists up a guy's butt? They stick their fists in up to here!" Ted indicated how far up on his arm this sex act entails. "Can you believe this?

I tried to change the topic, but it was too late. The

drag queens were laughing hard, tears ruining their mascaraed eyelashes.

"Ted, let's take a walk," I said, trying to get him off the porch to prevent further bursts of hysterics from the drag queens. Finally, he agreed.

The next day, I went to downstairs to the guys' apartment and found Dan, alone. I told him what happened, and he was laughing until he saw me—I didn't think it was funny at all.

"Dan, I feel awful. Like a double-agent. I have to watch every word I say in front of Ted. It's not right to do this to him—or me!" I was trying any angle I could think of to stop the lies.

"You have to tell him that you and Jaimie are gay. It's wrong. He thinks you guys don't include him when you go out because you don't like him. He is clueless."

Dan tried to joke it off, but it was not working with me. "OK, we will. We will tell him…soon. It's just so hard because Jamie and I know Ted will never speak to us again." Based on Ted's machoman bravado and his reaction to the magazine, I tended to agree that he was not going to take this very well. I did not share that gut instinct with Dan.

By the time I got back to the Seacrest that night from working a double-shift at Souvenir City, Ted had moved out. Dan and Jaimie were a little quiet around me for a few days, and then seemed to get back into their routine.

Ted told my parents that he was moving out because he and the other guys weren't getting along.

A few weeks later, I saw Ted on the Boardwalk. He was dressed in his Security Guard uniform and guarding an employee's only entrance at Convention Hall. He looked good, tan from spending more time on the beach.

"Hey kid, how have you been?" He seemed to be his usual friendly self.

"I'm good. Everyone misses you at the Seacrest. My parents and the guys." So did I, but left that out.

He shook his head and looked at his feet and then at me, "I don't care if they are gay or straight. They were my best friends. What I can't get over is the lie, and them thinking I was too square to understand." He insisted that the worst part was the lie and the lack of trust, not their sexual preferences. I wasn't convinced that he wasn't being honest with himself, but it's what he said he felt. The end resulted in a broken friendship, "what a tangled web we weave, when first we practice to deceive..."

"They really do miss you," I tried to explain.

"I miss them too, but right now all I feel is hurt."

I walked back to the Seacrest and was greeted by my mother in the lobby. She was rehanging curtains that she had washed.

"There you are. I made you a *luckshen kugle*. It's in the kitchen. Go eat, you look skinny!"

There was no way I was going to pass on my mother's

noodle kugle. Still warm, I devoured two slices of moist noodles full of fried onions. Next to her matzoh ball soup, kugle is my comfort food. Although I would never see Ted again, as I ate my last bite, I thought that Ted could probably benefit from a piece of my mother's kugle right about now.

Chapter Seven

Lamar & Damien

At the corner of St. James Place and Pacific Avenue, Saint Nicholas of Tolentine stood tall. Only six buildings west from the Seacrest Hotel, it was the oldest Catholic church in the area. The massive, grey stone architecture with its stained glass, marble statues, and mosaic interior looked more like a cathedral than a small city church. On Sunday during high mass, you could hear just enough of the Moller pipe organ's deep timber waft up the street like heaven was having a rock concert.

Saint Nick's, as the church was called, was named after Saint Nicholas of Tolentine, a 14th century monk who ministered the poor and criminals. Saint Nick was long gone from earth, but the sinning and confessing continued for centuries—stealing, adultery, and murder, just to name a few. The Seacrest had its share of sinners, and it's highly unlikely that there was enough holy water at Saint Nick's to purge the Seacrest of the confessions that its guests carried with them—if they even went to church at all.

Sinner or not, the front porch was always a pleasant spot for hotel guests. Even though you could not see the beach from the porch a half block up the street, guests would sit in rockers and enjoy the ocean air.

During the summer of 1976, the Bi-Centennial year, Lamar could often be found sitting, quietly and alone, on the rocker furthest from the front door. It was a busy summer; fireworks and marching bands to commemorate America's birthday brought many visitors to the city. Not that I was certain that was what drew Lamar to Atlantic City, or the Seacrest, but in any case, he became an almost permanent fixture for the entire month of July. He sat a lot—waiting for someone or something, in his platform shoes, and long, thick sideburns framing his dark skin and medium wild Afro.

There was much strangeness associated with Lamar. For example, he always had his "Super Fly" coat of polyester blends with him—light blue with dark blue stitching and a wide faux-fur lapel. Evenings at the beach may have called for a light jacket, but his coat seemed excessive for summertime. Maybe it was full of inside pockets to conceal items worthy of hiding.

Although his outfits were a bit over the top, what was

even stranger about Lamar was the fact that he did not live at the Seacrest. I wasn't sure why he first started visiting, but for months he would just come "hang" on the porch.

"Hello, Harry and how's it going today?" he would ask my father. "Would you mind if I wait on the porch for my friend?"

"You want to sit?" "Sure, as long as you are quiet, sit as long as you like." My father was too busy to care about why he tarried. Lamar was clean, quiet, and polite; for my father, those were some big selling points. Who knew who your next customer would come from, so a little good would never hurt, as far as he was concerned.

Lamar would come to the hotel and visit another Super Fly-like dude registered in Room 34. Like Lamar, Damien was not much of a conversationalist. But, to my father's delight, he was quiet, clean, and paid the rent on time—usually two weeks in advance and in cash. He didn't seem to have a regular job or schedule, but he had access to money.

Damien grew up in Atlantic City's Northside—predominantly Black neighborhood four blocks north of the Seacrest, tucked away from the tourists and Boardwalk. He told my father he went to Atlantic City High School, class of 1970. I was passing through the lobby one day and heard my father tell him that I went to Atlantic City High as well. Lamar didn't comment, and I kept walking towards the back of the front desk to my room.

Lamar would come see Damien a few times a day some weeks—or sit on the porch and wait for him whether Damien showed up or not. My father assumed they were in some kind of "monkey business" together, probably drug related.

Towards the end of July, Damien did not come back to the hotel. The room was paid for, so there wasn't anything to worry about. Presumably he'd show up. Lamar was always on the porch waiting—patiently.

One night, my mother went to bed in the room located off the lobby and right behind the front desk hoping to get a few hours of sleep. The room was technically used by my parents unless it was a busy weekend like July 4th and even that room would be rented. My room was down the hall and was never rented, not with my stuff—my beloved posters of Sylvester Stallone all beat up from the "Rocky" movie, and Bruce Springsteen and his E-Street Shuffle gang—I always had a permanent room to myself. My father used my room to stash the hotel earnings until he could get to the bank, and it was also where he did his paper work.

My mother, who always a good sleeper, woke up that night for some reason feeling like someone was watching her. To her surprise, huddled in the corner across from her bed was Lamar. Although the room was dark, the neon sign from the neighboring Hotel Shamrock shed enough light onto Lamar to identify him and his Super

Fly hat. My mother blinked a few times hoping she got swept up in a bad dream, but Lamar did not go away.

He put his index finger to his mouth indicating that he wanted her to be silent. My mother recognized Lamar as the guy who was always sitting on the porch. They really never spoke more than hello, but still a strange man, hotel guest or not, did not belong in her room crouching in a corner.

"What are you doing here?" my mother asked whispering, honoring Lamar's request to keep quiet.

"You know me, right? You've seen me around. You know I would never hurt you, right?" Lamar was barely audible.

"Please let me stay here a few minutes. Someone is out there looking for me and he will hurt me. But, I would never hurt you. I promise. Please don't get all upset."

My mother thought about his request and told him that she's sorry he is in trouble, but it did not make her comfortable to have him in her room as she hiked the light summer blanket from her knees over her waist.

"I understand, but you cannot stay here," my mother repeated calmly to Lamar still crouching in the corner of the room.

Simple, polite, and to the point. She really did feel bad for him, but a nice girl from a *shtetl* in Poland is not allowed have a strange man in her bedroom—not possible.

Lamar looked at his options. If he stayed, my mother might scream or cause a scene. So, he discreetly left my mother's room taking his chances. He apologized to my mother as he opened the door and repeated that he would never hurt her. She thanked him for leaving, and he disappeared.

A few days later, it was a weekday morning, and I was having breakfast with my parents. My mother took the opportunity since it was a slow day to make me *blinis*, thin and drenched in butter. How she could make a stack of paper-thin pancakes that were always the same size and thickness is something close to a miracle. My stomach always grumbled in anticipation when I heard her pour that batter onto the heavy skillet, buttered and hot. Those pancakes and a glass of chocolate milk was a breakfast dream for me—especially in the summer when my mother was busy cleaning and running the hotel.

I was just about to eat my last *blini*, drenched in maple syrup, when someone at the front desk rang the bell. It sounded serious, smacked twice, hard and no nonsense-like. My father got up and went to see who his next customer would be, and I followed since breakfast was over and I mostly had nothing better to do.

Two uniformed Atlantic City police officers were at the front desk as well as a man in plain clothes, stout and serious, who identified himself as Detective Prima.

"Can you open up Damien Brown's room for us, please," Prima asked my father, but his tone was more of a command rather than a suggestion.

My father asked if Mr. Brown (aka Damien) was in trouble which was at this point fairly obvious. since the ACPD was standing at the front desk. Detective Prima matter-of-factly told my father that Damien was dead, stabbed outside a bar in the North side of Atlantic City. The police wanted to go through his room to look for information about next of kin and anything that could give them some ideas as to why someone would want to stab Damien eight times.

My father got the master key off the wall of keys that he kept behind the desk and let the officers into Damien's room—well, what was once Damien's room. They looked around and found a few papers that Prima tucked into his pockets.

"What should I do with his clothes?" my father asked.

"Sir, if I were you, I'd toss all of this crap in the trash where he and his stuff belong." The other police officers laughed and headed out of the room—the sounds of their stiff uniforms rubbing against gun holsters and batons came with each step they took down the hall, keys clanging like Jacob Marley's chains in a *Christmas Carol*.

After the police left, my mother asked my father, "Dead? What do you mean dead? Oy, my God. He was such a young man. Who could do such a thing?"

My mother was not taking this news as lightly as the police took it. Shaken or not, she had a job to do—a room to tidy up. So, she promptly went into Damien's room and threw out what was left of his sparse belongings. He didn't have much except for some toiletries and a couple of shirts strewn carelessly over the twin bed. Then, she Lysoled the room until everything bad she could ever imagine drowned in that sick, thick smell. The room was small and she had it clean and sanitized to the best of her ability in about a half hour. Room 34 was ready for its next occupant.

The next day, *The Atlantic City Press* had a minuscule blurb about a stabbing at Fannie's Bar on Michigan and Baltic, but no motive was provided and no suspects were discussed. As for Lamar? He never came back to the Seacrest again.

Chapter Eight
Wendy

Wendy was white as in Caucasian, but just a slightly pinker version of the gauze-colored *shmattas,* as my mother would call it, that she wore around her head—a bland white caftan that wrapped her hair like one of the nuns in the *Sound of Music.* Her eyes were a once-upon-a-time pale blue, but more gray, faded, and tired.

Malik was always dressed in white with a round cap on head. His name was William Jefferson Brown, but he took the name Malik to make himself more Muslim sounding. Next to Wendy, his very dark skin seemed to make her look even more ghost-like. They lived in Apt #2—one of two small apartments on the street level of the hotel. Although the hotel rooms could be rented on a daily basis, the two apartments required a lease and monthly payments. Malik always paid on time, but what exactly he did to earn that money was never clear. Wendy had to stay home and was not allowed to work, Malik was the man of the house and his words were to be respected.

Wendy had a daughter from a previous relationship. Amy was about five and very sweet. She looked a lot like her mother only her eyes were bluer and her life had not yet been robbed and beaten into unhappiness. She had very long dirty blonde wavy hair. I guess that's what Wendy's hair looked like too. Who could know what was under the head covering and long caftan?

Almost immediately after they moved in, I could hear Malik yelling, presumably at Wendy. Often, I could not make out the words from the lobby area, but his deep, angry tone clearly conveyed rage. As the summer went on, I would hear the yelling more and more often. A symphony of one-sided sobbing sounds from a female and then a sobbing duet from mother and child. The occasional door slamming to add to the cacophony.

As the yelling increased, so did the visits from Wendy's mother. Usually on a Sunday morning, she would drive from her small rancher in rural Bridgeton, NJ where she worked at a glass factory ever since Wendy was born. Louise, always dressed in a very polyester, *haus frua* outfit. She always seemed uncomfortable with her almost son-in-law and his Muslim attire. They barely made eye contact with each other, but when they did, their faces would grimace.

Louise would fake a cough just to have an excuse to look away from Malik.

Jews, Catholics, and Christians had already been fighting for years for rights and equality in Atlantic City. The groups would set aside their beliefs to fight for a more important need for social and racial justice. Despite all of this, Muslims were excluded and rarely discussed, adding to the taboo notions surrounding them. A white and black Muslim couple was seldom ever heard of, let alone seen.

Louise seemed to take to my mother immediately with a "don't let this happen to your daughter" warning in her pale blue eyes. Born and raised in Bridgeton, Louise lived on the right side of the railroad track, the white and Methodist side. In the early 1950s when Louise was a teenager, "colored folks" knew their place, geographically as well as socially. Mingling with the other side was not permitted or tolerated. Period. Klan meetings in Bridgeton were less than secret, even into the 1960s when the KKK planned a membership rally in nearby Ocean City, NJ. Their motto was "the South shall rise again!"

Atlantic City held a history of fighting racism. While the rest of the United States was submerged in the burnings and riots of the 1960's, Atlantic City proudly debated race in the 1964 Democratic National Convention and kept many hotel doors open to all. In Atlantic City, unlike the burnings and riots of the 60s across the United States, racial tensions did not erupt, probably due to the iron fist that the North side lived by – AC was relatively quiet during the 60s.

As Louise carried her large body up the stairs from Wendy's ground floor apartment to the lobby, her chest heaved struggling for breath. My mother offered her a cup of coffee and her homemade *mandel bread* cookies. Louise accepted and they both went back to the kitchen. My mother put the water up and listened to her talk about her "baby girl, Wendy."

"I hate him," Louise blurted out followed by tears and nose wiping. "He beats her. That Black son-of-a bitch beats my baby girl. What does she see in him, he's mean and rotten. Black bastard, and what the hell is a Muslim, black Muslim?"

Nodding her head and offering more *mandel bread* my mother offered her opinion. "I don't know. He's not a Christian. He's not Jewish. I don't care what he believes in. There's only one God for all of us. The problem is why does he hurt Wendy?"

Louise sobbed out more insults about Malik. "Why the hell is he making Wendy wear long robes and wrap her head up like a nun. And the beatings. Why does she stay with him?"

My mother told her that she would try to help Wendy if she could, but Wendy rarely left Malik's side. Both my mother and Louise blamed him for the arrangement. Truth to tell, my mother didn't care much for him either.

He rarely spoke to white people—only if he had to and he usually preferred to speak to my father. He had a scar on his left cheek and angry, beady shaped eyes.

Louise dried her face and thanked my mother for the coffee, hugged her and asked that my mother call her if Wendy ever came to her and needed help. My mother told her she would keep an eye on Wendy and hugged her back.

As Louise walked through the lobby, she looked at me sitting on the couch. Then she put her hands together like it was time for prayer, looked up towards the ceiling, and said, "Please, Jesus, don't ever let this happen to Sonia's daughter too."

I did not hear any fighting coming from the apartment for almost a month. Wendy still looked sad and pale. A few times, when Malik went out, Wendy would come up and have coffee with my mother. Just one cup and run back downstairs before he came back to the Seacrest. I heard my mother tell my father that Wendy is scared to leave him and scared to stay with him.

"She's a nice girl," my father would argue for Wendy in her absence to defend herself. "Skinny and pale, but a nice girl. And those *shmattas* covering her head. Such a pretty girl. A *shandeh*."

"Yes, a *shandeh*, a shame," my mother would second that motion and echoed my father's words in Yiddish and in English. Although my parents always spoke Yiddish to each other when they were alone, they spoke English in front of guests for the most part. If my father got stuck for a word, he would revert to a Yiddish/English combination that seemed to work well enough to discuss towels, room prices, and check out times. When the family was alone, eating dinner or no guests in sight, Yiddish took over.

One morning yelling and cursing floated up to the lobby from Wendy's ground-floor apartment. Mr. Angeles, proprietor of the Shamrock Hotel next door, always kept a canvas sun screen lowered on the right-side of his porch to shelter his delicate clientele. He did not want the mostly blue-haired church going widows that had been coming to his hotel for the last 30 years to witness Seacrest Hotel comings and goings.

Mrs. Angeles would chat with their customers having iced tea with mint in matching glasses and refer to the Seacrest as vulgar. They could not see Wendy, but they heard Wendy's cries and they heard Malik's curses. Mr. Angeles yelled over from his porch to the Seacrest that he was going to call the police. My mother, holding a scrap of paper with a telephone number, was already in the phone booth in the lobby calling Louise.

Louise was about to leave for her job at the Kimble glass company in Vineland, New Jersey. She went to work there every day for the last 22 years wrapping and packing laboratory items like beakers, bottles, and, cylinders for scientists and classrooms all over the world. When she got my mother's call, she hesitantly called out from work. Louise always won the company's Perfect Attendance Award. There were only two times in the last 22 years that Louise did not receive the award. Once, when Wendy was born; complications arose and she was rushed to Newcomb Hospital for a C-section. And, now 20 years later, she would lose her recognition and $25.00 Sears card to help her daughter, or at the very least try.

Louise arrived 45 minutes later with Wendy's Uncle Jim and his pickup truck. ACPD was already there and one cop, older and a little overweight, walked Wendy out of the apartment and onto the street. She was crying and shaking. Her face was red and one eye shut and swollen like a prize fighter who didn't get the prize. Another cop was in the apartment talking to Malik. Guests from neighboring hotels gawked and tried to listen to what was going on at the Seacrest Hotel, yet again.

Louise ran up to Wendy and hugged her wiping the already drying blood with a hanky she pulled form her purse.

"No more baby, you are coming home with us."

"I can't Momma. I'm pregnant. Malik says it's a blessing from Allah." She fell to the ground as she said Allah's name. Louise helped to pick her up and quietly and calmly said to Wendy, "No. You are coming home with me—today." The police officer asked Wendy to press charges and Louise stared at Malik as he came out of the apartment. Louise put her arm around Wendy and held her tightly, "Do it, Wendy. We are taking you home."

Tears falling down her face, Wendy looked at the younger cop, grabbed Amy up into her arms, and meekly said, "Yes." The police jumped at the opportunity, cuffed Malik, and led him to the back of the squad car. From the car, Malik looked at Louise firing out a lengthy list of "fat White bitch" insults that made Louise smile.

"I'm gonna kill you, bitch!"

Louise kept smiling. She hated him and kept thinking of the school yard ditty of "sticks and stones can break my bones but names will never hurt me." Louise knew that if she could just get Wendy home, her tie to Malik would be cut, and Malik would never come to Bridgeton to find her.

Uncle Jimmy, who didn't say much, waited for Louise to tell him what to do next. Louise instructed Wendy to start packing up. She handed Amy to Louise, and immediately started throwing clothes and toys into boxes that Uncle Jimmy gave her.

My parents came downstairs and told Louise that the apartment was paid for until the end of the month—another week. Louise said she did not care and wanted Wendy out of Atlantic City as soon as possible.

Hugs were exchanged between my mother and Wendy. She apologized to my parents for causing so much trouble. They loaded several boxes into the truck and didn't bother to seal them.

"You take care of yourself—you're a nice girl," my mother said to Wendy.

"I will," Wendy said with more confidence in her voice than I ever heard before. "This time I really will."

The next day in the Atlantic City Press, there was a small blurb about an arrest at the Seacrest Hotel on 135 St. James Place—a William Jefferson Brown, charged with outstanding warrants including armed robbery and aggravated assault.

I told my father about the newspaper article. "Thank God. He was no good, a *bandit*. Let's hope he doesn't see light for a long time."

Chapter Nine

The Tea Cup Family

It was my last summer at the Seacrest Hotel. My parents sold the hotel the year before in 1978, the year the Gambling Referendum passed into legislation, to three guys who worked for the Atlantic City Electric company. They purchased the property as an investment—with high hopes of the land becoming the location of a casino one day. If they had a crystal ball, they would have seen that the Seacrest would not be gobbled up by a casino developer—ever—and still stands today as section-8 housing.

The new owners of the Seacrest hired my parents for two years to manage the place since they had no idea what to do in a hotel. As employees, my parents did not change the way they ran the hotel. In fact, the new owners, about 30 years junior to my father, would tell him on many occasions to "Take it easy, Harry" - a concept that was completely foreign to my father's full steam ahead work ethic.

1979 was also my first summer out of college. I was working at Resorts International – the first and only casino in town that year - in the Security Office as a Safety Deposit Box Clerk. It was just a boring summer job until I could figure out what to do with a degree in English and the rest of my life in front of me.

One night, I was working the 4-12 shift. There were three supervisors on duty overseeing about 35 guards on the hotel and casino floor. Right after the security supervisors radioed the guards under each of their commands to start rotating positions, two of the Supervisors returned to the office. Matt Stevensen, always polite and appropriate, came in first. The rumor circulating through the office was that Matt belonged to the KKK, or a similar kind of group in South Jersey. Appearance wise, he looked stereotypically Arian blonde and fair skinned. Some of the supervisors told me that Matt admitted to them that he was in the "club" and it was just a social gathering – nothing wrong or illegal at all according to Matt. As a supervisor, he was always fair to the Black security guards – ironically, never a single complaint was ever reported about Matt mistreating or harassing them.

Following behind Matt was Tony McGlynn, a retired cop from Long Island with a caustic sense of humor and a perpetually ruddy face. He plopped his large frame down next to me on the orange and brown two-person settee in the front of the office.

"Good golly, Miss Molly!" Tony's usual way to start a conversation with me.

I was expecting Tony and the other security guards to launch into a lengthy discussion about Steve Carlton's game the night before where the Phillies trounced his beloved Mets. To my surprise, Matt, who never said more than hello walked over towards me.

"Excuse me, Ma'am, I'd like to ask you to do me the honor of accompanying me to a wedding next month." He stood straight waiting for my reply staring through glass blue eyes.

The room got quiet, and I looked around to see if this was a joke. The other supervisors and guards did not laugh, and Tony mumbled under his breath, "Oh boy, this is going to be something." Everyone knew that I was one of the only two Jewish employees in the office, and then all eyes turned to me awaiting a reply.

"Are you talking to me, seriously?"

"Yes, I would be honored if you would attend the wedding with me." I was hoping a joke or something was coming soon, but Matt stood serious and obediently waited for a reply.

"Are you nuts? You want ME to go with YOU to a wedding with your friends?" What am I the entertainment at the reception? You going to throw me in an oven for laughs?"

Matt was taken aback and emphatically tried to assure me that they "don't do things like that anymore." I kept shaking my head in disbelief and then he informed me, "We are actually considering allowing your people into our organization."

I got up from the couch. "Matt, no thanks. I cannot go to the wedding, and keep your invitation to join your club as well."

He walked away and left the office, looking a bit deflated. The room burst into nervous laughter when one of the Black supervisors, who entered the room after the conversation started, blurted out, "Goddamn Ku Klux Klanners!"

Matt and I never had another conversation after that exchange. When my shift was over, I clocked out and walked the four blocks back to the Seacrest on the Boardwalk. I passed Central Pier – with rows of concession booths offering games like the one where you shoot water from a pistol into a hole that is a clown's mouth. As the water fills, a balloon on the clown's nose gets bigger and bigger. If you burst the balloon within the allotted timeframe, you would win a stuffed animal. As I heard the bell go dong because someone just won a 4-foot stuffed elephant, I remembered a time years before when I almost won a stuffed animal at that same booth.

It was the summer of 1966 , a boom season for Atlantic

City. For forty-three days straight during that summer, sixty percent of the airline industry was crippled when 35,000 workers went on strike. Airplanes went nowhere. It wasn't good for the airlines and their stock holders, but it was great for Atlantic City's hotels and restaurants, and even the Seacrest Hotel. If you can't fly, you find other ways to travel. And, the "World's Playground," as Atlantic City was once known, was a reasonable destination for millions of people in the Northeast to reach by car or bus or train.

One of the families that stayed one weekend at the Seacrest that summer had a daughter my age, Dorothy. We immediately hit it off, and played games in the lobby—9-year old kids could amuse themselves with a deck of cards playing Old Maid or Go Fish. Dorothy was very pretty—dark and perfect long braids crowning a round, cream-colored face that reminded me of coffee with lots of milk in it.

Although there were some proprietors in Atlantic City that did not rent to Black people even into the 1960s, my parents did not care about color. My father had two requirements—pay your rent on time and be quiet! Atlantic City, unlike other seaside towns, did not initially segregate its beaches and hotels until the 1900s, when white tourists coming up from Southern states complained about having to actually integrate with Blacks on the beach and in hotels. Many hotels acquiesced and started refusing to serve Blacks, Jews, and other groups deemed undesirable. Many

Blacks around the country, and even in Atlantic City, began staging stay in protests at white hotels. By the 1930s, the *Negro Motorist Green Book* held names of hotels owned by and catering to Blacks. These hotels flourished in the Northside of Atlantic City, an 80-square block section of the city, along with clubs, stores, and restaurants—like a scaled down version of Harlem in New York City.

In the afternoon, Dorothy's parents asked my mother if they could take me on the Boardwalk with their daughter to go on the rides on one of the piers. I jumped up and was ready to go, looked at my mother for approval, and was thrilled when without any hesitation she said, "Of course." My father gave me a few dollars as spending money, and off we went.

Since my parents ran a hotel that made ninety percent of its money during the summer, our family never did summer vacations. So, when Dorothy's parents took me on every ride on Million Dollar Pier that they thought appropriate for our age, like the Rocket Ships and the Twirling Tea Cups, I was thrilled. We ate pink cotton candy, and played Skee-ball - an arcade game where Dorothy and I barely were able to roll a ball up an incline into bullseye rings. If you got the ball in, you got points. Points got you tickets for prizes. She, with the help of her father, earned enough points to get a three-inch-tall Teddy Bear. I tried my hand at the concession booth where you shoot water into a clown's mouth through a water pistol – I didn't pop the balloon, and did not get a prize, but Dorothy and I had a great time trying.

We then walked 10 or so blocks on the Boardwalk and went to Steel Pier. Inside the pier, we watched Disney's *That Darn Cat* in one of the movie theaters, and outside, we were mesmerized by the Diving Horse act; a trained horse with a young lady on its back leaping from a 40 feet tower into a pool of water four times a day, seven days a week until the late 1970s when animal right activists shamed the act out of existence. Dorothy and I had a fabulous day eating and playing on the Boardwalk.

The day was fairly young when we left the hotel, but by the time we returned that night it was late – around nine o'clock that night. When I walked into the lobby with Dorothy and her parents, my mother looked a bit strange – relief and fear all in the same expression. She politely thanked the family for taking me out and we watched as they took Dorothy up to their room for bed.

I plopped down in my bed and reviewed my perfect day in my head. I overheard my mother on the phone talking to one of her friends, Mrs. Levi. She was informing her that I was home safe and sound. I had never heard that tone in my mother's voice before – like a child who had been chastised.

"I never thought to ask the parents when they would be back," my mother pleaded her case. "I know, they are strangers. Yes, I should have asked more questions."

Mrs. Levi went on and on bruising my mother and berating her for her parenting skills. She insisted that she would never have allowed her child to go with strangers. I could tell my mother was exhausted and was ready to concede just to end the prattling. Finally, I heard my mother cut her off with a final word.

"OK, I was wrong not to ask questions. She's home now. They are a nice family. It doesn't matter that they are a *schvartze* family - that part doesn't matter. Enough already with their color."

The next morning, Dorothy and her parents checked out. It was a warm summer day, the family was nicely dressed; mother and daughter in a matching light pink cotton dress with a white straw hat and the father in a seersucker suit with shiny, white shoes.

Dorothy and I hugged each other and asked if we might see each other again next year. Her parents smiled, "We will see if we can, dear."

Before they left the lobby, Dorothy's mother gave my mother a gift to show how much they all appreciated their stay at the Seacrest Hotel. After they left, my mother opened the box. It was a lovely china tea cup and a saucer, porcelain white with delicate blue flowers, carefully wrapped in tissue paper.

We would never see Dorothy and her parents again. My mother loved the gift and cherished it. Over the years, when she dusted the cup, she would hold it in her hand

and retell the story about the nice family and how Mrs. Levi berated her for allowing me to go off with *schvartzes* on the Boardwalk. That teacup was displayed in her china closet for 50 years until my mother sold her apartment and moved into assisted living.

Some things should just not matter.

Chapter Ten

Joe, George, and Jim Morrison

Exactly one day before July 4, 1971, Jim Morrison died in a bathtub in a Paris hotel. I was fourteen years old and my exposure to Morrison and The Doors mostly came from the two guys playing his records in Room 25. From *LA Woman* to *Riders on the Storm* to *Mr. Mojo Rising*, Morrison's voice was like a siren to me. Calling and calling, but at 14, I was not quite sure what I was being called to. I did know that I liked the sound and the lyrics, and more importantly, I liked the from-the-gut singing and Morrison's bad boy attitude. A few years earlier, although I was only 10, I distinctly remember The Doors on the Ed Sullivan show singing "Light my Fire" in 1967. The song, as did Morrison himself, seemed out of place next to clean-as-a-whistle

Ed Sullivan regulars like Robert Goulet and Topo Gigio. Morrison was mesmerizing.

Music, like psychedelic posters, was exploding in the late 60s, and having an older brother gave me an in as to what was the "groovy" new tune. I would "borrow" Saul's albums when he was not home, he had everything from James Taylor to Iron Butterfly. Luckily, he never found out, or was just nice enough to look the other way.

In the summer of 1969, Atlantic City hosted a music festival to over 100,000 hippie type kids, just a few weeks before Woodstock. The Atlantic City Pop Festival lasted three hot days in early August and boasted over 30 bands, including The Byrds, Canned Heat, and Joni Mitchell. My brother, who at the time was already in college, went. I was only 12, but I really wanted to go too.

"Please. Pretty please, take me. I won't say a word. I won't bother you and your friends," I pleaded to deaf ears over and over.

Even when I enlisted my mother to ask on my behalf, the answer was still no. "Take your sister, what's the big deal?" Unbeknown to me and my mother, the big deal was sex, drugs, and rock n roll—all not suitable for a 12-year-old little sister. Although I did not go, Saul did bring back souvenirs for me like a braided wax candle and a strobe yo-yo. With the help of a battery, that yo-yo would flash different colors when you rolled it up and down—I thought that was the coolest thing on the planet. For days after the concert, I heard my brother and his friends talk about the festival like Joe Cocker spastically singing "With A Little Help from My Friends" and the crowd going wild dancing to The Chambers Brothers doing "Time Has Come Today." In addition to the souvenirs that Saul brought back from the festival, he also gave me his ticket—a prize I still have and cherish.

Joe McNulty and George Kopek, the guys in Room 25, worked on Central Pier for the summer operating amusement rides. Joe usually worked the "Hell Hole" and George split his time between the "Tilt-a-Whirl" and the Ferris Wheel. They were both juniors in college, Pennsylvania boys, attending Penn State. Together, they decided to work in Atlantic City to make some money and sneak in some fun at the beach. The Seacrest was a half block off the Boardwalk and Central Pier—one reason they decided to live at my parent's hotel. The other being that it was inexpensive compared to a better class hotel, only $25 a week for both of them.

Joe was gregarious. His flaming red hair with slight waves and a scraggly beard gave him the appearance of an Irish pirate. He was a ladies' man, and would often watch females as they walked by. He had an adorable wink that girls his age loved. In Atlantic City, he met most of his dates at work, where he would have plenty of time to flirt with girls, often dressed in elastic tube-tops emblazed with Foxy Lady logo and hot pants barely covering their butts as he helped them onto a ride. When they exited, he would close the sale.

"So, ladies. Foxy ladies. Wanna go get a beer at the Irish Pub once I get off of work?"

He was always warmly smiling, exuding a politeness hammered into him from years of Catholic school. He seemed like the kind of boy a girl could bring to meet the folks, but the devil himself dwelled happily beneath his exterior. This approach usually worked in his favor when he prowled for girls.

Their favorite band was the Doors and Jim Morrison was their hero. Joe and George saw them in concert several times. Room 25 was stacked high with records, turn-tables, and speakers that they brought from home. Like Joe, Morrison was a bad boy with an angelic face.

One of Joe's favorite stories was the day he slapped a nun across the face. And, for the most part, he got away with it. As he told it, he was seven years old and trying to be the center of attention in Sister Magdalene's second grade class. Joe was imitating George Reeves as Superman on the then popular television series, by flying from chair to chair during recess. Sister Magdalene was not amused and clearly saw a straight line to hell from children watching that "electric box filled with devils." The ancient nun, covered by a huge very black habit, only had her face exposed. He described her skin like Elmer's paste, emphatically lined with ripples of wrinkles, and very annoyed at Joe's actions. She grabbed him by the back of his hair in the middle of his fly-by. When Joe stopped, he twisted around, and Sister Magdalene slapped him in the face, telling him to stop his nonsense.

Joe recovered immediately from the sting on his cheek and his classmates' bewildered stares. He brought his little hand up and gave the nun an Old Testament eye-for-an-eye pay back. Sister Magdalene was shocked to have been slapped back, and even more so by a little child. Joe took the opportunity to kick her while she was down, "You are in so much trouble, Sister. My Dad is gonna be really mad when I tell on you!"

He was sent home that day from school for his bad behavior, but Joe was back and gloating the next day. His father, it turns out, was the mayor of his small town outside of Pittsburgh, and had significant clout in and out of the local church. Sister Magdalene begrudgingly apologized for her actions and Joe returned to class as long as he promised not to play Superman in her presence ever again. Joe thought that was a fair price to pay, even if it was only for a few minutes.

When the news broke on television that Morrison was dead, Joe and George did not go to work at Central Pier. They both called out sick to pay their respects. For what must have been twenty-four hours straight, Joe and George took speed, as crystal meth was commonly called, and drank beer, all the while listening to the Doors' music on repeat.

I went with my mother to check on them when she and my father did not see them leave for work. She knocked on the door, "Boys, are you inside? Are you feeling all right? I have chicken soup, if you are sick." Joe opened the door and gave my mother a hug. "No, Sonia, we're not sick. We lost a good friend. He died." George showed my mother an album. She shrugged not knowing who Jim Morrison was.

She looked at Morrison's picture. "I feel sorry for his mother—he's a young boy. Oy, what's going on in the world these days," she lamented, asking again if the boys needed her chicken soup—a cure for most ailments.

I visited the guys several times that day because I liked them, and they were sad. Even though I was just the landlord's kid, they let me hang around. Many nights I would go visit them at the Central Pier and they would put me on a ride and leave me dangling over the jutting pier for twenty minutes. I loved it—suspended hundreds of feet off the ground with views of Atlantic City—sometimes upside down, depending on when Joe or George would shut off the ride and leave me floating. If I got hungry or bored, I just yelled down to one of them and they'd start up the ride—gears cranking away as I descended back to earth.

They had built a shrine on the bureau made from empty beer cans, with two of their albums, *Waiting for the Sun* and *Morrison Hotel* prominently displayed. The shape was pyramid-like and a large patchouli candle, placed in the center of the shrine, burned as the record player spun its non-stop eulogy. The mirror on the bureau was covered with a poster; a bare-chested Morrison extending his hands out either trying to hold on to dear life or trying to drag you into his downward path. The interpretation was left to the beholder.

Although George was the quieter one of the two room-mates, he felt the need to perform. He recited the "Lizard King," tears streaming down his face, when I walked into their room.

Once I had, a little game
I liked to crawl, back in my brain
I think you know, the game I mean
I mean the game, called 'go insane'
I am the lizard king
I can do anything

Joe was thirsty and popped open a can of Bud—it was only 11:00 in the morning—and yelled out,

When I was back there in Seminary school
There was a person there
Who put forth the proposition
That you can petition the Lord
With prayer
Petition the Lord with prayer...

When Joe got to the last line of the lyrics, he was red-faced from shouting—angry, hurt, and frustrated. To me, he sounded very much like Morrison, belting out

"You Cannot Petition the Lord with Prayer." It seemed religious-like and appropriate for a Jim Morrison memorial.

The next day Joe and George reluctantly went back to working the rides on Central Pier. After a week or so, Joe brought back a girl to the hotel that he met at the Irish Pub. She said she was anxious to see the shrine that was erected in Morrison's memory. She was one of several girls in August to make the pilgrimage back to the hotel with Joe. The shrine stayed intact until they moved out of the Seacrest in early September and went back to school.

Chapter Eleven

Lionel

At the Seacrest, I had my own room. It was at the back of the hotel behind the front desk; a small nook with a single bed and a tall, two-door green metal closet for my clothes. The bed butted up to the one window facing a wrought iron fire escape—black and chipped with age. Sometimes, for fun, and a little change of pace, I would ask my parents if I could sleep in one of the empty rooms. They would never agree to this on a weekend or the week of a holiday, but on a slow weekday, they would usually give in if I promised to clean up the room in the morning.

After selecting a room that my parents approved, I would grab the key with the green oval Seacrest Hotel plastic fob hanging from the rack behind the front desk, and spend the night in a "hotel." Some kids played house; I played hotel. It was fun to mix it up and sleep in a new room—crisp new sheets, different furniture, and a different view. Since there were no TVs in the rooms, I would just look out towards the Boardwalk or read a book or magazine until I drifted off. It wasn't the most exciting thing to do, but it passed the time.

I loved room #44. It faced the Boardwalk and the beach without any other buildings to block the view, and gave me a birds-eye view of the city. The sea breeze used to sneak in through the windows on windy summer days with hints of warm pretzels and salt water taffy. I used that room the day the Traymore Hotel was imploded in 1972. It was a gorgeous old place with that old-world château kind of look and feel. In the 1920s, it was a classy place to stay for the highbrow and wanna be high brows with money.

In its heyday, those who were deemed respectable were treated like royalty at the Traymore and other luxury hotels. Like the neighboring Dennis Hotel on Michigan Avenue and the Boardwalk and the Chalfonte-Haddon Hall located a few blocks away closer to Steel Pier. If you were not the right kind—and by that I mean no Blacks and no Jews—you needed to find a room elsewhere, anywhere but not with the WASP crowd.

A friend of the family, Dr. Stan Fleishberg, would often tell me about his first memory of Chalfonte-Haddon Hall in 1946. He was 10 at the time, it was one year after the war had ended. The Fleishberg Family decided to spend a hot summer weekend in Atlantic City. His parents wanted to get out of Queens and enjoy the beach and Boardwalk. When the family arrived at the hotel to check in, a staid front desk clerk looked Stan's father straight in the eye and ever so politely informed him that there were no longer any rooms available. When Mr. Fleishberg reminded the clerk that he had a reservation, the clerk tilted his head slightly towards the front door and said without emotion, "Very sorry, sir. The hotel is full. However, many people of your faith seem to enjoy the Seaside Hotel around the corner. Have a good day."

Mr. Fleishberg was furious. He grabbed Stan by the hand and the family left the lobby and checked into the Seaside without any problem. Although the Seaside was a very nice hotel, a 10-story building in a Spanish colonial style, it was not as grand as the Chalfonte-Haddon Hall. It was also not their choice to stay there—it was forced on the family. After an early dinner, Mr. Fleishberg suggested a movie at the Steel Pier, right across the Boardwalk from the Seaside.

When Dr. Stan would retell the story, he would always say that he "remembers the movie they saw that night like it was yesterday." The movie, *Crossfire*, a film noir drama dealing with anti-Semitism starring Robert Young, hit very close to home that night for the Fleishbergs. As a result, Dr. Stan never forgot his first trip to Atlantic City.

When I was a teenager, prejudice was very much alive and kicking in Atlantic City, even if it had become a little less obvious. At the Seacrest, as far as hotel rules went, it was non-existent. My father's only rules, "don't make noise and pay your rent," trumped your race or religion. He was not interested in your politics or your beliefs. He was there to make a living; an honest living renting rooms to customers, regardless of their skin color. Although he knew all too well what it felt like to be singled out and abused by Poles, Russians, and Nazis because he was Jewish. From name calling in the school yard to organized pogroms to mass murder, my father took abuse without ever expressing the need to return the sentiment.

Although my parents were technically Polish—their families had lived in the area for generations—they were always Jews first. Antisemitism was rampant and virulent. Poland contained the largest Jewish population in Europe and was the center of Jewish culture for many centuries. but the Poles took every opportunity to reinforce the idea that they would never be true citizens.

My mother would always add, "We all pray to the same God—why can't we all get along?" There was never an answer to her rhetorical question. She always got along with all sorts of people of all backgrounds. In her later years, she would shop at Trader Joe's, sometimes daily. On one occasion, I went with her. As soon as we entered the store, she was welcomed like a rock star. Employees smiled, waved, and knew her name, and she knew theirs. As we headed down the frozen food aisle, she was suddenly hugged by a young Muslim woman wearing a hijab. She grabbed my mother and wanted her to say hi to her mother who was working behind the free samples counter. The three of them chatted for a bit, hugged good bye, and we continued shopping. She always had that effect on people.

One evening, as I sat in the lobby watching TV, a summer rerun of *All in the Family*. I think Archie was in the middle of insulting Meathead, his son-in-law. I noticed out of the corner of my eye a man talking to my father about room rates. At first, it sounded like basic negotiations. He introduced himself. His name was Lionel and he was beginning to get testy, not at all like Carroll O'Connor's homestyle Archie jabs.

"Come on man, give me a break. I can pay ya $20.00. That's it."

"Listen," my father calmly explained, "I don't have any rooms for that price July 4th weekend. Next weekend, yes. All hotels are higher today. Go check next door at the Shamrock Hotel. Same answer."

"You ain't renting to me cause I'm Black, that's why."

"That has nothing to do with nothing," my father explained. And he meant it. *Gornisht funn gornisht!* He grew up in Poland where there were no Blacks and no discussion of hating a man because he was black skinned. Irrelevant. Never came up. Just like now.

Lionel kept hounding my father to find him a room at a rate that he thought was fair. He was in his mid-20s with an Afro twice as big as his head and his easily six-foot lean physique was getting more tense by the minute. Then, he mumbled under his breath, but loud enough for me to hear something about "goddamn cheap Jews." I knew my father heard him loud and clear as well.

Lionel looked at me, searching for an ally in his absurd reasoning that he was entitled to a cheaper room because he wanted it and because he was Black. Of course, how could he know that I was the owner's daughter, not a hotel guest. I flew off the couch and was in Lionel's face yelling at him even though I was half his size. No one was going to talk to my father like that.

"Are you a complete idiot? Did you miss history class about the American Revolution? July Fourth is a holiday—for all of us—and we all pay extra for rooms on special weekends no matter what color you are. Get it?"

Lionel looked at me and then my father, realizing that I was not coming to his aid. On the contrary, I kept telling Lionel over and over that he was wrong. He just stared at me with a look that could be interpreted as a giant question mark. My father told me to calm down. *Genug shain!* He kept saying in Yiddish that it was enough and to let it go—turn the other cheek when confronted with prejudice. Growing up, my parents taught me to be friends with all people—any religion or background. But, they also emphasized that I needed to be careful of who I was friends with. How could they not tack that message onto their lessons? Based on their experiences, when bad times or circumstances arose, Jews were always the scapegoat. My parents told stories, over and over, about Christian friends and neighbors in Poland that turned on Jews in a heartbeat during the war, willingly and enthusiastically.

Unlike my parents, I did not grow up with openly Jewish hatred like they did in Poland. There, it was best to keep quiet if a gentile made a slur, if you wanted to live or not get beat up, at the very least. Behave and take it. But when I heard Lionel degrading my father and my religion, I instinctively protected my father. When I was a child, I would love watching *Hogan's Heroes* on TV—I would often understand a German word or two, like *shnell*, since it was similar to Yiddish. I was 9 years old and could never understand how those bumbling idiots on the television could have murdered my family and millions and millions of other families. When the kids in the neighborhood would play *Combat*, another TV show in the 1960s, albeit more realistic and not a spoof, I insisted on playing Sgt. Saunders every time so I could machine gun as many imaginary Nazis that I could—I needed to save my family. That moment in the Seacrest when I saw an attack, an affront on my father, I jumped up. Lionel backed off.

"Never mind. I don't need none of this."

He strolled out mumbling something about taking his business somewhere else. That sounded just fine to me. When Lionel left, I expected to get a pat on the shoulder from my father as he came out from behind the front desk. Instead, he called the guy an idiot, a *bullvan*, and told me not to yell at customers any more, even if they were idiots. My father was much better equipped to deal with anti-Semitism than me.

"A *meshugeneh velt*," my father lamented about the crazy world in general or maybe just that night at the Seacrest. He went into the kitchen behind the front desk and made himself a cup of strong tea in a glass with two sugar cubes and a teaspoon of my mother's home-made sweet cherry preserves. He stirred the glass several times mixing the preserves evenly through the tea. As soon as the tea cooled off enough to drink but still be hot, he took a big sip and exhaled with a sigh.

Chapter Twelve

Bart

Unless your name was on the Seacrest Hotel registration card, you were technically not permitted to go up to a room. Only registered, and therefore paying guests, were permitted. This basic rule was to prevent one person registering and then having several friends or family sleep in that room, a common practice.

A single room without a private bath ran $15.00 a week; a double room with a private bath was $25.00.

Guests checking in had to complete a 5x7 card and fill in pertinent information like name, address, and telephone number.

There were boxes available for make of vehicle and license plate, but, most guests at the Seacrest did not come by car. Greyhound was the common mode of arriving into

Atlantic City bus terminal followed by taking a transit bus, cab, Jitney bus, or walking.

No matter how they arrived, "Smith" was a very common name on the registration card for guests at the Seacrest. Usually no relation to each other, circumstances and situations made them all part of one big, not necessarily happy family. One night (or afternoon) stands, affairs, and other situations that echoed the line from the 1960s TV show, "There are eight million stories in the naked city..." The Seacrest kept its fair share of them.

For every rule, there is an exception. And for my father, Bart was the exception to who was and who was not permitted to go upstairs. I am not sure why Bart was the winner of my father's leniency; maybe he reminded my father of someone he admired from his youth. I don't really know. When I first met Bart, I thought he looked a bit like Cory Negron from *Three Dog Night*. You could almost imagine Bart breaking into song, *"Mama told me not to come...that ain't no way to have fun, son..."*

Bart was handsome, but a complete jerk. When he was in the lobby, he would always check himself out in the mirror hanging over the couch facing the front desk one time too many and just a second too long admiring what he saw in the mirror; preening is curly mane of black hair and his Fu Manchu mustache.

He grew up 45 minutes up the Atlantic City Expressway in Cherry Hill, New Jersey. At twenty years old, he was going into his junior year at Rutgers, majoring in Business Administration and then law school. He decided working for the summer as a waiter in Atlantic City would be a great way to make money. Most people, specifically girls, thought he was cute—great hair and blue-grey eyes, with long thick lashes. He could be charming, and he knew it.

Waiting tables at The Ranch House worked out well for Bart as a summer job. The restaurant was only a five-minute dash from the Seacrest to the Boardwalk—an important feature for Bart since he almost always was running late. He made pretty good tips, but as you might imagine, managed to meet lots of girls as well. Many nights Bart would bring a girl back to the hotel. Since my father was behind the desk waiting for the next customer to check in, day and night, and awake, on most occasions, Bart would have to walk into the lobby and have some kind of conversation with my father before heading upstairs with his new girl.

"Hi, Harry. How's it going?" "Good, good. And, you?" my father would ask, a smile already planted on his face.

Not even waiting for a response to his first question, my father then would point to the giggling girl standing next to Bart. "And, who is this?"

"Harry, this is my sister," Bart would reply with a devious twinkle in his eyes. Usually, he would stand behind the girl, so she could not see him putting his finger up to his mouth motioning to my father to please *Shhhh*.

"Sister? Again? Oh boy, you must have a big family."

My father would tease Bart and waive him on. Never a single lecture about the rules that only registered guests can go upstairs.

One afternoon, I was sitting on the porch. It was my day off from work at the souvenir shop on the Boardwalk. Bart usually ignored me since I was just a 15-year-old to his mature 20 years of experience. He ran up the front steps of the porch, two stairs at a time, and noticed me sitting on the porch.

"Hey kid, what's going on?"

"I'm good," I replied not understanding why he was being so chatty. My immediate thought was he wanted me to do something or get something from my father to somehow benefit him. Because we never really talked to each other, I was a bit suspicious.

"No, I can tell. What's up? You look like you're in deep thought about something? Is it about a boy?"

I shook my head. No, I just had some stuff on my mind.

"I'm good at this. I have two sisters at home. I know you have something bugging you. Come on spill"

I did have a dilemma I was trying to resolve, but now was distracted by the fact that Bart noticed and genuinely seemed to care. He sat down next to me in a rocker, pulling it up close to mine.

"Well, I was invited to a party tonight and I am not sure if I should go or not," I started to explain, a little embarrassed that I was telling Bart, of all people.

"OK, why are you not sure if you want to go?"

I told him the story, reluctant at first but then feeling a bit cathartic actually getting it off my chest. Roadies for the rock band, Bad Company, came into Souvenir City where I worked and purchased lots of "head" supplies; rolling papers, pipes, a bong, and other paraphernalia. They were performing two nights at Steel Pier. The $2.25 admission to the Pier included the headliner show, two movies, and more. Bad Company was headlining that week. In the past, names like Louis Armstrong, Frank Sinatra, Rolling Stones, and the Supremes, to name a few, performed on Steel Pier through its 70-year history.

The store had an eclectic offering of merchandise ranging from souvenir ashtrays in metal or glass, T-shirts with any logo you can imagine, to a 79-cent deck of nudie playing cards stamped with "Greetings from Atlantic City." I usually worked the T-shirts counter or stocked shelves with new arrivals of tacky souvenirs that tourists would gobble up. The store was plastered in Day-Glo pink signs with hand written descriptions and prices in runny black paint which seemed to scream, "This crap is cheap. Come buy me!" We could barely keep the shelves stocked on most weekends.

The older guys, as in over 21, at Souvenir City, worked behind the head supply counter located in the back of the store. When the Bad Company roadies came in, they immediately hit it off and they invited all of us at the store to a party in their suite after the show.

"So, why don't you want to go?" Bart asked.

"Well, I am only 15, but it sounds really cool, and everyone in the store is going."

"*But?*" Bart interrupted.

I tried to explain to Bart what was going through my head. I wasn't quite sure if I wanted to hang out with strangers—older guys—years older than me that were going to be high as kites. I trusted the guys I worked with, they were not that many years older than me. Most of them were like big brothers. It was the big time, rock band roadies that I didn't know and couldn't decide if I wanted to trust them. This would be a party to remember, lots of sex, drugs, and rock n roll, at least I suspected! Part of me wanted to go to the Deauville Hotel where they were staying, and part of me knew not to go when I was only 15.

"Listen, kid. I am not going to tell you what to do. Party sounds like it's going to be wild. What an opportunity to party with the band."

"So, I should go?"

"That is up to you. But, I gotta tell you that I really admire you. You're a smart kid for even stopping to think instead of just jumping into this. I'll see you tomorrow. I want to hear what you decided to do."

He got up, tussled the top of my head, and ran up to his room.

I took a long walk on the Boardwalk, purposely

avoiding the souvenir shop. As I passed one of the Gypsy palm reader's joints, a part of me thought of going in and getting some "spiritual advice," but I knew better. Rather than waste my dollar on a phony fortune teller, I debated between a cut of chocolate Steele's fudge, homemade on the Boardwalk daily, or a cone of Kohr Bros ice cream. I passed up both options, and just headed home since it was close to dinner time anyway.

When I got back, my mother had dinner ready. She made pan-fried hamburgers and her homemade French Fries, which were each the size of a door wedge. It smelled wonderful, even my father sat down at the table, actually leaving his position at the front desk. We three ate dinner together that night since it was a weekday, and not a busy night.

"Eat another hamburger—you look skinny. People will think I am poor and can't feed you," My father pleaded, putting, another helping on my plate.

"OK, pass the ketchup."

The burger was juicy, full of *gribinez,* fried-to-charred onions. Everything tasted just right. Midway through my second burger, I decided not to go the party.

When I went to work the next day, a couple of the guys were dragging, still hungover. They told me I missed a great party and regaled me with details of all the drugs that were offered. One of the guys began joking, alluding to something about an orange and the Bad Company hit,

"I'm Ready for Love," and what one of the roadies did with it. Despite my curiosity, he refused to let me in on the particulars.

As I went out to the front of the store to put batteries in the mechanical dolphins that spun around in a tub of water—a big seller at Souvenir City, it occurred to me that I was glad that I didn't know about the orange.

Chapter Thirteen

Eamon's Record Collection

In the early 1970s, Irish college students flocked to the USA, specifically to tourist towns like Atlantic City to work summer jobs. Ireland, torn up from economic and political strife, did not offer much to their students. Traveling to America and working the summer not only provided them with a way to make some money, but a chance to travel, and most importantly, get out of Ireland's bombings and unrest. Some arrived from Belfast, and others from Dublin. After a while, you could actually distinguish them from their accents, and especially their attitudes—usually easy going and upbeat from Dublin, and belligerent and suspicious from Belfast.

Although many Atlantic City hotels and businesses rented to and employed hundreds of Irish students, Catholic sounding St. James Place seemed to be the unofficial epicenter for the Irish visitors. The Seacrest sat on the half-way mark on one of Monopoly's orange properties, St. James Place—right next to her sister colors on the game board, Tennessee and New York Avenues. The street bookended with St. Nicholas Catholic church, referred to as the Atlantic City Cathedral, at the corner of St. James and Pacific Avenues. Since the early 1900s, the magnificent church served the large population of Catholic residents in the city as well as thousands of tourists. The church is one of the most ornate buildings in the city. To this day, St. Nick's adorns the city with stained glass windows, marble statues, and a turn of the century Moller pipe organ; which on occasion when the grand doors were left ajar, I could hear from the porch of the Seacrest Hotel. On the opposite end of St. James Place, right before you walked onto the Boardwalk, stood The Irish Pub. In between, small rooming houses and hotels rented to packs of Irish university students that came to America for the season.

The Seacrest had about a dozen students living there for the summer season—usually two sharing a double room without a private bath for $20.00 a week. On their days off, they would sit in the lobby watching American TV. They looked forward to laughing at Irish Spring soap commercials where a young, bucolic couple frolicking at a riverside smell the bar of soap and exclaim, "And, I like it too!" Apparently, the American actors had lousy Irish accents according to Eamon and Tony, two of the Irish guys who would mock the words over and over.

The two were roommates at the Seacrest in Room 35 and were college "mates" back in Dublin. Eamon, short and wiry, was the outgoing one next to Tony's tall, thin frame and more serious demeanor. Next door to them in Room 33 was Sean and Patrick, Belfast boys. Any night when they were not due to work early the next morning, the pair joined their friends at the Irish Pub for a pint or two or three. On many occasions, you could hear them coming down the street after leaving the pub, breaking bottles, cursing, and punching parking signs. When they got to the Seacrest, they attempted to sober up their act, probably in respect to my father.

"Good evenin', Harry!" They would stumble and giggle as they entered the lobby. They were often very inebriated, but always trying their best to be polite when they saw my father perched at the front desk. My father would waive them on keeping the conversation short encouraging the boys to get to their rooms and settle down.

"OK, boyez. Looks like you had a good time," my father would comment. "Now, go up to your room to sleep. You have work tomorrow. Shh!"

Sean would go over to the behind the desk and pat my father on the back as the other guys climbed up to their rooms, "Harry, you're all right, y'ar!"

Eamon always had his finger on the pulse of what he

thought was only possible in America. For example, he was absolutely fascinated by the "blue water in the john." My mother would place plastic tabs in the tank, Ty D Bol, that turned the water in the bowl blue as a cleaning method after every flush. Eamon never saw this product in Ireland. He would lift the lid in the shared bathroom on his floor and announce with pride, "Jesus, I luv this country..."

He also figured out how to get "free" record albums for himself, and all the other Irish kids staying at the Seacrest. In most any magazine and in the Sunday papers, there were ads for the Columbia Record Club. For only one cent and the five minutes it took to fill out the form, the deal was too good to be true. Columbia would send you 12 records, of your choice, for a penny. If Eamon, or one of the other guys bothered to read the fine print, they were then obligated to buy an agreed upon number of albums in the next 12 months at regular price. Since they would all be back in Ireland by then, Eamon only adhered to the large print part of the deal.

Eamon, Tony, and the other guys started filling out the Columbia forms pretty regularly using variations of their name—and then the boxes of records started arriving at the Seacrest. Watching the guys open box after box filled with albums was too tempting. I decided to join as well. After carefully inserting the penny into the pre-cut slat and completing the form, it took about two weeks until my box arrived.

From Carly Simon's *No Secrets* album that rocked the charts with "You're So Vain" to Rod Stewart's *Every Picture Tells a Story* and the unforgettable "Maggie May," my record collection improved by 12 in one day. Unlike the Irish guys, I took the small print pretty seriously and bought my obligatory albums over the course of the year. When Eamon and Tony went back to Ireland after the summer, they left me the albums they could not manage to pack into their suitcases or had duplicates of. One of them, Santana's *Abraxas* album with hits like "Black Magic Woman" is still in my vinyl collection—a memento from Eamon and his Columbia Record Company scam.

For the most part, the Irish kids from Dublin hung around with other kids from Dublin; and the same with the Belfast gang. I never saw any blatant animosity from one group to the other, but the two sides of Ireland usually went about in their separate ways. Like any rule, there's always an exception. That summer at the Seacrest, Kaitlin and Brendon took that title. The couple, who met at Trinity College usually kept to themselves because Kaitlin was from Dublin and Brendon from a small village outside of Londonderry. The young couple, who were a few years older than the other Irish kids, had already graduated from college. Brendon wanted to continue his studies to become a veterinarian like his father who specialized in farm animals serving neighboring villages near their home. In addition to being a vet, Brendon's father, Doc

McKenney, was politically active and a fierce supporter of the IRA and independence from England. Brendon kept his relationship to Kaitlin a secret, and so did Kaitlin to her family—neither family would accept anyone from the "wrong" side.

Kaitlin was shy and quiet, which was probably her nature, but also a symptom of living a discreet and secretive life. She warmed up to my mother and they would sit and have tea together when Kaitlin was off from her housekeeping job at Haddon Hall—a classic hotel on the Boardwalk that would become part of Resorts International Hotel & Casino, Atlantic City's first, five years after Kaitlin made their beds. She had long and thick brown hair that came to her waist. On her days off, she would untie the braided bun and let her hair flow loose.

My mother tried to encourage her to talk to her mother, assuring her that a mother would understand "anything about her child." I am not sure if my mother really believed that or was just trying to get Kaitlin to talk to her mother – give her a chance even if the odds were stacked against a happy ending. Kaitlin missed her family. She was torn about her need to keep her relationship a secret from parents who were adamant that the IRA was nothing but a "pack" of murders and thugs hiding behind alleged political reasons.

Once a month, she would call her mother from the pay phone in the lobby with a handful of coins. She would ask about her little brother and Pa. There was a little bit more of small talk and then the coins would drop into the box indicating that the call would end quickly unless more coins were added.

"Sonia, you don't understand how much our families hate each other. I can't tell them about Brendon. He can't tell his family about me. That's why we decided to stay in the US." Kaitlin, cried as my mother hugged her, and informed her that she and Brenden were never going back to Ireland after the summer. Kaitlin wasn't sure when she would ever see her family again.

My mother would tell my father and me about the young couple and their troubles, usually at dinner when we had some time to ourselves. My father thought they were a nice couple—quiet and polite; never drunk and rowdy like their other Irish countrymen.

"A *rachmones*," My father would comment feeling pity for Kaitlin and Brenden, but also for their parents. Not being able to ever see family again was a reality my parents knew all to well after Nazis murdered their families—brutally, cold, and systematic.

After the summer, Kaitlin told my mother that they were moving to Chicago. She had an uncle there who supported them and would help them figure out how to stay in the country - my mother seemed relieved to hear they had a plan. She poured my father another glass of hot tea and spooned in her home-made strawberry preserves to sweeten the taste. My father was about to dip a piece of *mandel* bread into his tea when someone banged the bell at the front desk. He took a sip as he stood up, and ran off to check in a new guest.

Chapter Fourteen
Kennie Kerr

Kennie was the "nice lady" in room 12 who would bring my mother flowers every Friday afternoon. When she checked into the Seacrest at the beginning of the summer, casually dressed in tight bell-bottom jeans and a clingy tube top, she told my parents that she was a "performer" at one of the gay clubs on New York Avenue, next street over from the Seacrest. She smiled politely explaining to my parents that she wanted a nice, clean room with a private bath. She also wanted to be able to just "hop over" to the next block to easily go to work. As she leaned into the front desk discussing summer rates, she turned her right hand over her shoulder and pointed her index finger towards New York Avenue, with her bright red nail polish adorning her long, thin fingers.

I never really got to know Kennie. She would smile and wave to me, but clearly, she adored my mother. She slept during the day time so she could perform late night shows, 10:00 PM, midnight, and the 2:00 AM late show on summer weekends, but always made time to see my mother. Even when Kennie's friends from the club would visit her, introducing my mother was a must. Joey, a drag queen friend of Kennie's with a lean runner's body and dark brown doe eyes, would come over to the Seacrest so the two could hang out. I would hear them coming down the stairs and Joey insisting that they say hi to Sonny, their pet name for my mother.

"Sonny, I just love your new blouse," Kennie would always compliment her. One day she gave my mother some hot pink nail polish that Kennie thought would go better with my mother's complexion. My mother thanked her even though she would not polish her nails, with any color let alone hot pink, during the busy summer months—too much work to be done to keep up manicured hands. My mother gave her a hug and told Kennie she loved the color and handed her a bag of homemade *mandel broit*.

Although my mother must have known at some level that Kennie was a man, she always referred to him as she. Perhaps it was his nightly theatrical exit from the lobby in a long black wig and a beaded gown, bright red with a touch of silver, that persuaded Sonia. I don't think my mom had ever heard the 1971 hit by the Cornelius Brothers and Sister Rose, but she did her best to "treat her like a lady."

A drag queen must have been a strange concept to a *shtetl* girl from Poland, but my mother didn't seem to care. Regardless of his excessive use of lipstick and other cosmetics, he was a customer, paying and quiet. This was a lesson she learned in America—the customer, no matter how *modneh* or odd, is always right. My mother had never even heard of or known anyone in the old country that was a homosexual. She would tell me on many occasions, "We didn't have this in Poland, maybe it was possible in Vilna or a big city, but not in my little Miory."

I never discussed such things with my father, but I am going to guess that he probably heard talk about men who had sex with other men. Growing up in Poland, he went to a Hebrew school, *cheder*, every day until he was 13. No doubt his *rebbe* covered Leviticus 18:22—the who you can and cannot lie down with section of the Old Testament. *A man shall not lie with another man because it is an abomination.* To my father, that may have been true, biblically speaking. But, if you did it quietly and paid the rent, who was he to judge if you were a woman wearing pants or what gender you decided to lie down with.

When my parents bought the Seacrest Hotel in the early 70s, New York Avenue, the next block over, was known as the gay street in Atlantic City. It was ground zero for gay customers of every flavor. Atlantic City, true to its resort beginnings in the 1880s, accommodated anyone's whims and wishes, legal or illegal, from drinking and gambling to forbidden trysts of any shape and color.

In the 1920s, New York Avenue offered one hotel that accepted gay clientele—hush, hush. By the time the 1960s arrived bringing power to the people—women, homosexuals, Blacks, and anyone listening to Beatles crooning, "You say you want to have a revolution...,"—the entire block was alive and kicking openly for gays, lesbians, drag queens, and anyone else in between. Upscale hotels like the Chester Inn, Mama Mott's Italian restaurant, bars like the Saratoga, and several night clubs open to gay and straight clientele flourished on New York Avenue. Even underground circulations of gay magazines from Philadelphia and New York City raved about the discos, drag queen competitions, and gay hospitality of New York Avenue.

The light bulb went on for my mother in the early 1970s, when she figured it out. I was sitting in the lobby one afternoon watching *General Hospital* since I had just walked back from Atlantic City High School, my sophomore year, and did not feel like doing my French literature homework just yet.

My mother was on the phone, with her *yenta* friend, Sylvia Holtzman. She enjoyed talking to her friends, almost all of them were fellow Holocaust survivors. They would chat and gossip for a bit, but my mother would get her fill quickly. Unlike Sylvia, my mother could tolerate talking about other people's woes for just so long, and then she politely would say she has to go because a customer needed her, even if there was no one in the lobby. We did not have a private phone in the hotel and used the lobby pay phone as our personal phone. The gold spray-painted booth gave the illusion of privacy, but anyone sitting in the lobby could overhear every word spoken, despite the overhead fan that ventilated the booth with a bumble bee-like buzzing that rattled through the entire lobby.

I tried not to listen, but it was nearly impossible. I gathered from my mother's half of the conversation that Ida Kaplan's daughter, another Holocaust survivor family from Poland transplanted to the Atlantic City area, was in college in Syracuse, New York. She was dating a gentile guy, a *goy*. This, for most if not all Holocaust survivors, was a bitter pill to swallow. They had survived Hitler and his attempt to destroy the Jews of Europe. Now they learned that raising children in America meant your kids would not necessarily live by the old rules. It was an adjustment, to say the least, that my parents struggled with; wanting their children to fit in, but not fit in so well that they lose their sense of uniqueness and being different.

My family and I spoke Yiddish in the house and kept a kosher home—no *traif* allowed. The path I was sup-posed to take was clear; go to college and then marry a nice, Jewish boy. It was direct and straightforward. Some Holocaust survivors demanded it of their children with no exceptions and others, with broken hearts, learned to accept the new world ways they were thrust into.

"So, Ida is upset?" my mother asked Mrs. Holtzman in Yiddish about poor Mrs. Kaplan. I could not hear the reply, of course, but no doubt she replied with "*Voh dehn*?"—Yiddish for what else could she possibly be.

My mother slid open the folding doors of the booth to let in more air. As a result, I could hear Mrs. Kaplan's high-pitched voice coming through the phone. Continuing with her lament, Sarah was dating not only a gentile, but a "*schvartzer*" as well. Mrs. Kaplan continued with one *oy vey* after another about the tragedy the Holtzmans were dealing with—their daughter dating a goy that was a black man.

Interracial dating was an emerging social oddity in the 1970s—only a few short years after the Supreme Court ruled laws prohibiting mixed marriages as unconstitutional in 1967. My parents never came out and made a formal announcement that my brother and I should *Not* marry a black person; it was just assumed that we would marry a white Jew—preferably someone with Holocaust survivor parents with similar likes and dislikes, *landsman*. To my surprise, my mother took the opportunity to reply to Mrs. Kaplan when she finally stopped to take a breath of air, "Well, at least he is a man. What difference does it make if he is black? Let me tell you what is going on these days. Girls go on dates with girls." My mother then proceeded to tell Mrs. Holtzman about the concept of homosexuals, which she is quite confident, did not exist in Poland before the war. At this point, I was all ears and listened intently to my mother telling her friend all about the people and couples in the hotel. I am not sure if she comforted or shocked Mrs. Holtzman. But, one thing for sure, my mother introduced her to a whole new set of rules. She suddenly became the knower of things unknown to fellow *shtetl* girls that survived the war and made it to New Jersey.

Yes, what is the world coming to and yes they look happy and maybe they are right…which led to a series of discussions about heterosexual couples they both knew, here and back in Poland, that were not happy. My mother set her entire community straight (no pun intended) about a new world, *"A nayer velt—a maidel mit a maidel, an ingel mit an ingel…"*

If I could have arranged a musical accompaniment, it would have been perfect to have the Kink's singing,

"Girls will be boys, and boys will be girls
It's a mixed-up, muddled-up, shook-up world
Except for Lola"

Every Friday afternoon Kennie would come to the lobby and call behind the front desk for my mother.

"Yoohoo, Sunny are you there?"

My mother would come out, chat a bit, and thank Kennie for the pretty flowers. She would arrange the carnations and baby's breath in a tall glass vase, clear with a scallop rim on the top. She placed the flowers next to the *Shabbat* candles that she would light in our small kitchen tucked away behind the front desk. The sign above the kitchen door said *Proprietor Only*. It was a place for some privacy for our family, with a nice touch thanks to Kennie Kerr.

Chapter Fifteen
Sal

One summer weekend, friends of mine from Rutgers came to visit me at the Seacrest Hotel. Sal and Michael were an item, and Sal was a former crush of mine from college.

When I met Sal in 1975, my freshman year, he was a sophomore engaged to his high school sweetheart back in Woodbridge, New Jersey. His fiancé, Eve, waited patiently back at home until her man got his diploma before they would marry and have 2.5 kids and live in a suburban development in Jersey. She even had a hope chest, a large cedar Lane one, packed with quilts knitted by her granny and a Waterford vase left to her by an aunt who passed away. These were only some of the items in that big box of soon to be burst expectations. Sal's junior year at Rutgers would end up being memorable to Eve in a very rough way.

In the dorm rather than study for our exams, Sal would always interrogate me about Atlantic City and the gay street off the Seacrest Hotel. He seemed to be fascinated with the city and the fact that my parent's hotel was close to New York Avenue. On my bulletin board, hanging over the bed in my dorm room, I posted a black & white glossy head-shot of Kennie Kerr in full drag. Kennie lived at the Seacrest and performed nightly on New York Avenue. Not sure why I displayed his picture; maybe to shock some people and maybe to gauge who was open and cool and who was not.

Sal picked up on it immediately, asking me lots of questions about what I thought about transvestites, homosexuals, and what it's like to live in that environment. I thought it was idle curiosity. And, since I was a sucker for boys with gorgeous blue eyes, girl-like long lashes, and dark waves of black hair, any conversation would have worked for me. I was not the only female who noticed Sal's good looks and charming smile. He always had a date that he selected from a bull pen of willing girls around campus on the weekends when he didn't go home to Eve. He built himself a well-deserved reputation of being a cad—a big man on campus.

As he and I spent more time together, chatting about the different people that lived in the Seacrest, Sal must have realized that I was not going to be gaped mouthed about gay people. Unlike some of the other people in our dorm, especially frat boys and wanna be frat boys, someone's sexual preferences did not concern me. Years of interacting with all sorts of people at the Seacrest just made me accept what some people might label as odd and weird, at best.

After a few months into the semester, Sal confided in me that he was gay and that he had a lover, Michael. They met at the frozen custard store where Sal worked, at the Paramus Mall, on weekends and holidays, for about a year. Michael, who was in his early 30s, owned that store and several other franchises in North Jersey. Sal's ladies' man bravado on campus was just that, a way to ensure that none of us would suspect even for a minute that he was leaving campus whenever he could to spend time with his male lover.

By the end of Sal's junior year, he dropped out of college to help Michael run the custard franchises. He moved in with him in Michael's beach house in Deal. Sal's parents were disappointed about his decision to quit school—the first in the family to go to college. They were confused and lost about his sexual preferences, his mother lit candles to St. Anthony expecting an answer she never got. Eve's heart was broken.

One weekend the summer after Sal left Rutgers, he and Michael drove down to Atlantic City for some vacation time and visiting me. They booked a week at The Chester Inn on New York Avenue, a very nice hotel that catered primarily to gay clientele. After they checked in, they walked over to the Seacrest. It was great seeing Sal again and we sat in the lobby catching up on who was schtupping who back at school—although a Yiddish expression, it was one of Sal's favorite acronyms for having sex.

As the three of us chattered and giggled, my father sat behind the front desk and ignored us for the most part. Occasionally, he would shoot me a glance and his forehead would wrinkle with a *what can possibly be so funny* expression as Sal and Michael critiqued every fashion faux pas that walked in and out of the lobby. Although my father had a good sense of humor, he was serious when it came to work and workplaces. Slap-stick humor like the Three Stooges never made sense to him. He also poo-pooed professional wrestling labeling it "such fakers," but would on occasion, enjoy watching a boxing match on TV.

In the winter, when he had more time away from the Seacrest and would watch television, he and my mother would never miss a Saturday night of Lawrence Welk— especially the Lennon Sisters singing away and never dropping their wholesome as apple pie smiles.

If he watched one of my shows, like *Laugh In*, my father would often times not get it—something got extremely lost in translation. He would watch a few minutes, impatiently, as *meshugeneh* actors like Artie Johnson rode on toy tricycles or Ruth Buzzy banged her pocketbook on an old man's head. My father would sigh and then leave the den to go read *The Forward*, his favorite Yiddish newspaper, at the kitchen table. As he left the den, my father would look at the TV and shake his head and say in Yiddish, "There's just not enough rope in the world to tie them all up, that's why some of them are running around loose." That was his usual ending comment when he couldn't explain a person's odd behavior.

Sal, Michael, and I were discussing what show we would attend that evening when a woman came down the stairs and walked over to my father. I never saw her before, and assumed she was at the Seacrest for the night or a weekend. She was quite stout, manly in her body shape, and dressed in rolled up jeans at the ankles and a flannel shirt loosely covering a protruding belly. Her hair was short cropped and without style. She smiled at my father and leaned into the desk whispering something to him. He nodded and said "of course" very softly and went into a storage area behind the lobby. When he returned, he handed her a small paper bag, neatly folded down to about 5 or so inches high. I didn't have any idea what my father gave her and why it was in a bag, but the three of us sitting in the lobby observed the transaction intently—like a dog watching for his master to open the dog treat bag and reveal the goodies.

Sal was curious, he wanted to know what was in the bag and why they had to whisper. That was Sal, always inquisitive and wanting to test new waters. He and Michael planned to travel extensively in the next few years to exotic places; hike Machu Picchu and snorkel in Galapagos. He always wanted to have a full cup of whatever life could bring him. Drink it to the last drop, and fill it again.

Marked bathhouses and public bathrooms were popular hook up spots for gay men and served as a sanctified place to engage in secret affairs and act on passions without judgement. In less than 10 years, Sal would die from AIDS contracted from one of the many encounters he had in these public bathroom stalls because Michael was not enough. Free love would eventually collect its due from Sal in 1987.

Nudging me on, Sal kept asking, "Come on, let's go ask your father what she wanted." I was curious as well since I never saw my father wrap things in paper bags, so we got up and walked over to the front desk. When I asked my father what was in the bag, he told us that the woman asked for toilet paper. "Why did you put it in a paper bag?" Sal asked.

"Vy? I tell you vy—when the lady whispered what she wanted, I figured she was a genteel lady and I didn't want to embarrass her with a roll of toilet paper."

Sal, screamed with laughter and that earned a very stern look at me from my father. He kept repeating "genteel lady" over and over until he could compose himself, wipe the tears caused by excessive laughing off his pretty face. He would retell that story about my father, the paper bag, and the genteel lady for years every time I saw him.

That was what you got at the Seacrest—full service no matter what you were or were not. Unlike Sal, my father did not notice that the woman was "butch" and what that may imply. He noticed a woman who demurely whispered toilet paper and thought it would be proper to put a personal product in a bag. Just a Seacrest amenity for any and all of her guests.

That same night, I went to a drag club on New York Avenue with Sal and Michael. It was a full-house; lights dimmed and the spotlight lit up the elevated stage. Kennie was just gorgeous as he pantomimed a Chorus Line fav, "What I Did for Love."

In his red beaded gown, he was a hit sparkling with each exaggerated gesture and gyration. His ruby lips puckered up as he began with "Kiss the day goodbye..." I was mesmerized by his performance and too many Black Russians that Sal was buying me throughout the night. Being one of the only females in a place where you are surrounded by 100 gorgeous men passionately kissing each other was a humbling experience. I was non-existent. Although I was without testosterone or a penis, I felt welcome to stay.

After two Black Russians and the sparkling disco ball

lights refracting in all directions igniting the faces and bodies that filled the room, I looked around and realized that I had been at a gay bar five out of seven nights that week with Sal and Michael. I had not spoken to a straight man in a week except for my father and my boss at work at the souvenir shop on the Boardwalk. I was not dating anyone at the time and was not even interested in anyone—after Sal confided his sexual preferences to me a few months prior and burst my bubble. So, I turned to the guys and shared my vodka-fueled revelation.

"Hey, I think I must be gay. Do you think I am gay?"

Sal looked at me with those gorgeous eyes and asked for an explanation. I told him that I basically seem to only be surrounded by homosexuals, so therefore, I must be too. No?

He put his arm around me, gave me a big kiss—oh what I would have given for that at the height of my crush—and said, "Honeydew, look around. You are the only girl here. If you were gay, you'd be across the street with the ladies at the Brass Rail. No, you are not gay. You are a little drunk."

Sal's succinct interpretation of the evening was all I needed. The thought of being a gay person never crossed my mind until I mentioned my observation to Sal who nipped that concept right then and there. Although I never questioned my sexual orientation ever again, I still remember Sal's twinkling eyes and giggle when he "straightened" out my conclusion of what it meant to hang out in a gay bar with him.

I thanked him for putting my sexual preference questionings, albeit brief, into perspective and resumed focusing on Kennie prancing around on-stage lamenting loves lost.

The applause brought down the house as he raised his long arms draped in a black feather boa and belted out the last "Can't forget, can't regret what I did for love."

Chapter Sixteen

The Guy in Room 17

As I left the Seacrest for work, the TV in the lobby was covering the week-long story about the arrest of David Berkowitz, Son of Sam, a serial killer who terrorized and perplexed New York city for over a year leaving eight people murdered and at least seven others wounded. My mother and several hotel guests were intently watching *Good Morning America* as TV host David Hartman explained that Berkowitz, after police and psychiatrists interviewed him, confessed that his neighbor's dog instructed him to do the killings. I waved good bye to my mother, and she lifted her head away from the TV just long enough to say, "Bye bye, call if you will work late."

I started working at Souvenir City, only one block away from the Seacrest on the Boardwalk, when I was in high school. I continued to work there during my breaks from college as well. Not that it made the headlines of the *Wall Street Journal*, but I single handedly broke the glass ceiling at Souvenir City by being the first female stock person. Until my *Ms Magazine* fueled moment kicked in, house rules were clear—cashiers were girls only and boys did stock. I did not want to be trapped behind a cash register all day dealing with other people's money. When I was 15, my first summer at the store, I convinced my manager, Frank, who was only 2 years older than me, that I refused to be a cashier. I insisted on equality in the souvenir store. He agreed pretty quickly, and history was made! Putting batteries in a mechanical fish swimming in a baby pool in the front of the store, stocking shelves with the crappiest souvenirs on earth, and selling head supplies to hippies, were some of my many duties as "stock girl." Gloria Steinem would have been proud of me.

I didn't have to be at Souvenir City that day for another half hour, but I left the hotel a little earlier to walk on the Boardwalk and briefly say hello to my school friend Grace – she was working at Ryba's Fudge shop where Mr. Ryba would make and mix and form acres of fudge on a marble slab table in the store window. The shop was only two blocks from my souvenir store and I had just enough time to visit with Grace and smell the chocolate and sugar whose scent seemed to melt into your clothes. Grace was handing out samples that day, and I continued on to Souvenir City with a mouthful of freshly made chocolate walnut.

When I got back to the hotel around six – tired from a busy day at the store and looking forward to dinner, two ACPD detectives announced themselves in the lobby. They asked my father to look up one of our guests – Rodney Morrow. I vaguely remember what he looked like. My father referred to him in Yiddish when he spoke about him to my mother as the *clainer* – the short one. I had seen a young Black man, about 5, 2 with a huge Afro coming and going from the Seacrest. His hair, picked out to its fullest, still did nothing to give him a taller appearance – even with patent leather platform shoes that John Travolta would have envied in *Saturday Night Fever*. Rodney was very much like many of the Seacrest customers – kept to himself unless he needed to pay rent or wanted an extra towel.

My father retrieved the green metal box of registration cards and pulled out the card for Room 17. The detectives looked it over and then asked my father if he would open the room.

He obliged, sans warrant, since growing up with Stalin and Nazis left my father with no concept of legal search and seizures, Miranda, and other rights the average Joe is entitled to in America. My father often talked about the Russian army that invaded Poland from the East in 1939 and helped themselves to homes, farms, and anything deemed valuable for the Communist cause. My father watched his business seized and his home assigned to a greedy Russian Commissar. Even as a child, I remember my father railing against the Communists and their invasion of his land – and even in America, decades later, he was vehemently against all Communism whether Ho Chi Minh, Khrushchev, or Castro

By the time the Poles, Jewish and non-Jews, came to grips with the Russian annexation of Eastern Poland and my father sweating each day in fear that he would be sent to a Siberian gulag for possessing one too many cows, Hitler broke his agreement and invaded the Soviet Union. Poland was seized by the Germans and within a year, the Nazis would be well on their way to exterminating nearly 2 million Polish Jews.

When the ACPD detectives asked my father for help, he obliged. After all, they were not there to "take" anything away from him – with or without a warrant. He was happy to accommodate what he felt was a simple police request. I stayed in the lobby to man the desk as my father escorted the police upstairs.

When they left, my father filled me in that the police were looking for Rodney. He told the detectives that Rodney had paid in advance for a week in cash, and the last time he remembers seeing him was two nights ago. They didn't explain why they were looking for him, and my father didn't ask. One of the detectives handed my father a card and told him to call immediately if Mr. Morrow returned to the hotel.

Since Room 17 was paid up by Mr. Morrow for another two days, the room was technically occupied even though its occupant was apparently nowhere to be found. After three days, my mother, who did most of the housekeeping tasks for the hotel, went up to clean out the officially vacant room. When she was finished, she collected Mr. Morrow's few possessions, mostly clothes and shaving supplies, in a black trash bag. She also found a small, well-worn valise tucked under the bed.

I strolled into the Seacrest a little after midnight, with the main purpose of getting a snack out of the fridge, something that my mother had prepared and left for me—a plump cheese blintz or maybe her stuffed cab-bage. Either would be appreciated since a Kohr Brothers swirled custard cone was all I had eaten the entire night on my 15 minute break away from the T-shirt counter. I chose the blintz. My head was buried in the fridge looking for the sour cream when my father asked me to step into a small room—actually more like a closet for supplies and fresh towels and sheets.

"Come with me, I want to show you something," my father said to me in Yiddish. I took my blintz and followed him.

The room always smelled fresh from the newly starched laundry. My mother was very clear about the cleanliness factor at the Seacrest—no matter how much DNA and body fluids were collected on her sheets, the professional launderers took the bags of soiled stuff and miraculously returned them with bleached clean and pressed supplies.

My father pointed to a small suitcase on a shelf and asked me to open it. I clicked the brass-like button that released the clasp and looked at the inside. I blinked and for a second, I felt like I was in a drug deal scene from *The French Connection* movie. Channeling Gene Hackman playing Popeye Doyle, I carefully inspected the quality of the product. The case was jam-packed with clear plastic baggies full of white powder neatly stacked two layers deep—lined up like a department store display.

"Vell, what is it?" my father asked with a good idea that the answer would be something illegal.

"It's heroin or cocaine." I told my father that by looking at it, I could not tell which one it was.

"What do you think this is worth," my father asked. Not with intent to sell purposes, but just out of curiosity. He always wanted to know more than his 8th grade education level from pre-War Poland provided. My father was always curious and inquisitive and wanted to learn about anything; utility stocks, Henry Kissinger, and the need to defeat Communists. My father would always say that a person must always learn and grow—that only a *bahaymah*, a cow, thinks only of eating and chewing its cud. A human needed to be better than that.

I took a guess that it was heroin, but told my father that I'd have to show it to friends who had a better idea. Although I would not indulge in any white powder, I knew people who did and would be happy to tell us. Hard drugs have been popular in Atlantic City since the 1920's when Al Capone met with the crime lords of the city following the St. Valentine's Day Massacre in Chicago and agreed to stop shootings and promote gambling and drugs instead. The two vices thrived and fed off each other developing a reliance on heroin and cocaine by the 1970's.

"Vos gayt on duh?" My mother caught us. Not that we were doing anything wrong, but when she asked what we were doing, my father and I were a bit startled.

My father assured her that we are not going to touch or sell the drugs, "God forbid." Just having a conversation. She obviously did not approve of our conversation topic, delivered a loud and disgusted "Feh," and slammed the suitcase shut.

My father found the detective's card at the front desk under some mail. He took a dime out of the metal cash box to call the police from the pay phone in the lobby. The detective who answered the phone told my father that a squad car would be at the Seacrest shortly to pick up the suitcase full of drugs. My mother looked relieved and asked me if I wanted another blintz that she offered to heat up for me. I agreed, and of course plopped some sour cream on top.

I Met a Man on the Internet

I t's not what you think. I was not looking for love nor searching in all the wrong web places like match/harmony/datemeplease.com. No, I was minding my own business when I got an email from a complete stranger who read one of my short stories on the web. Although I am nowhere near twenty-something, I, like many of my generation, regularly use the Internet and various social media outlets like Facebook to "hook up" with friends that I have lost throughout the years.

Have you ever asked yourself, "Hey, wonder what ever happened to Tony?" Well, now you don't have to wonder. You just Google or friend him, and voila, Tony is found. He's gained an unflattering twenty or thirty pounds and has collected several wives along with numerous children since you had a crush on him in high school. You know where he lives and that his second ex-wife contributes regularly to Our Lady of Mercy church. It's amazing, you used to need to hire a private detective to find this much juicy dirt. Wonderful stuff!

However, the Internet and all its superhighway options also lets people find you, and that takes us back to the man I met on the web.

Let's call him Joe. Apparently Joe read one of my short stories about the Seacrest when my parents owned it. As I've explained, the Seacrest Hotel was a colorful place, to say the least - pimps, prostitutes, and transvestites regularly made up the guest list.

Joe reached out to me because he worked at the hotel when he was a teenager. He must have Googled me to find a site that posted my email address and sent me a long (by email/Twitter standards), wonderful email about how he came to work in Atlantic City for a summer, what he did at the Seacrest, and his memories of the Boardwalk including Mr. Peanut and the Waffle Guy.

I was thrilled to read his email --I love AC and stories from the seedier side of the Boardwalk. He also mentioned that the owners were Polish Catholic immigrants and that they had a daughter. He was wondering if that could be my family and me.

Although there is only one Seacrest Hotel (it's still standing today on St. James Place), something was wrong with Joe's story. First of all, my family is not Polish Catholic. A Jew could be born and raised in Poland, but would never really be accepted as true Pole. Second, we never had employees working for us. So, I re-read the email and checked the dates. Joe worked at the hotel in 1968. That was about two years before my family bought it. I never knew much about the Seacrest prior to when we lived there. I was a teenager and by definition too dumb and disinterested to care about history and nostalgia.

So I wrote back to Joe and explained that my family owned the Seacrest from 1970 to 1980, after he worked there.

It seemed quite a strange coincidence to me that Polish immigrants owned the Seacrest twice in its illustrious history. And, that they had a daughter too.

My writer's brain started to wander. Did Joe have a thing for the hotel owner's daughter? Was she the love that got away? Or, was Mrs. Polish hotel owner his forbidden love? Perhaps his Mrs. Robinson-ski? Was Joe using the Internet to find a lost love from 1968? Well, probably not, but, it was fun to let my imagination run wild!

I asked Joe if he had any pictures from his days at the Seacrest. He did not, but said he did have a few items that he would send to me. Now remember, Joe was a mystery, and I didn't know was to expect. Would I actually hear from him again? After why should he go out of his way for someone he has never met and likely never will?

To my great surprise, about a week after our email exchange, a Priority Mail package arrived for me.

At first, I thought it was something I bought on eBay (Atlantic City nostalgia stuff is my weakness). I soon realized it was from Joe. He sent me a treasure chest of Seacrest memories: hotel stationary, a business card from the previous Polish owners, and last but absolutely not least, a post card of the Seacrest Hotel – linen finish, color, probably from the late 40s, and in perfect condition.

I was having a particularly poopy day when Joe's package arrived and it just lifted my spirits 10 miles high! Not only did he send a piece of Seacrest history that I had never seen before (didn't even know any post cards of the place existed), but I was touched by the gesture. Joe did not have to do that – it could have sat on his desk for weeks. I guess Joe is not a procrastinator. I like that in a person I don't know!

Anyway, I have since framed the post card in a double-sided clear frame so you can see the front and back. It's sits on my coffee table – a cherished memory that just warms my heart and nostalgia gene every time I glance at it.

So, Joe, thanks for being such a great stranger, brief email companion, fellow lover of the Seacrest Hotel, and an inspiration to me to write more stories about the hotel on St. James Place.